Mardle and a Troshin' in Norfolk

"Ten months of my Life" - 3rd Edition

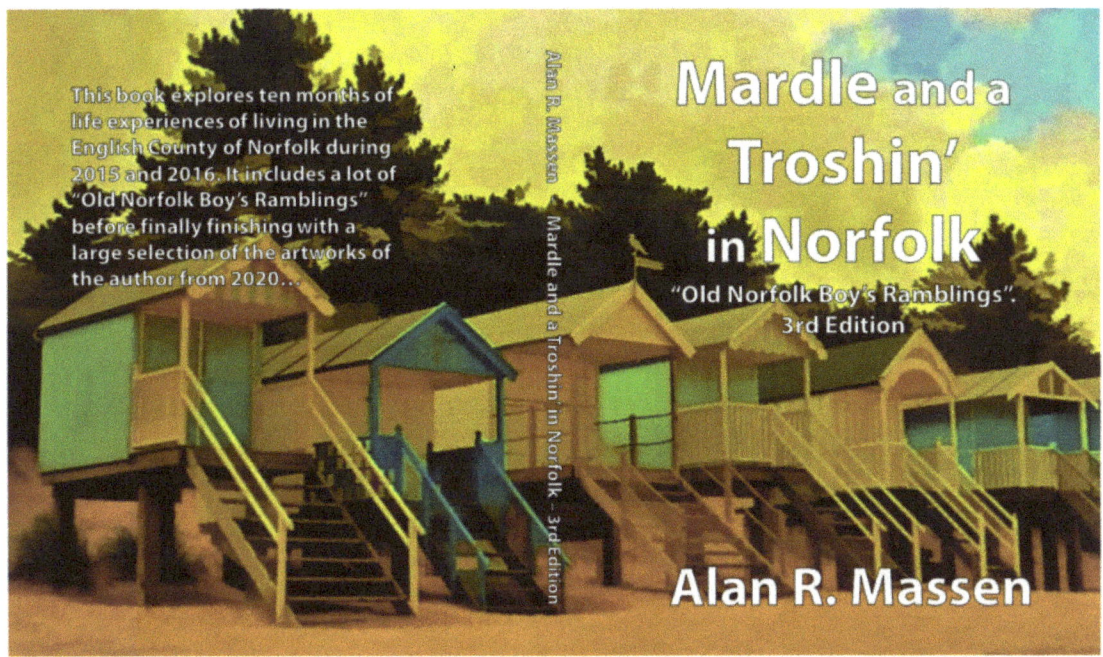

A Journey exploring ten months of living in the English County of Norfolk and beyond by recalling the authors life experiences from July 2015 to April 2016 explored in words and pictures before finishing with artworks by the author from the year 2020.

"An Old Norfolk Boys Ramblings".

by Norfolk Watercolour Artist Alan R. Massen
Published by Rainbow Publications UK

First Published in 2016 by Rainbow Publications UK
2nd Edition Published in 2019 by Rainbow Publications UK
3rd Edition in 2020 by Rainbow Publications UK

Copyright © 2020 Alan R. Massen

The moral right of Alan R. Massen to be identified as the author of this work has been asserted in accordance with the UK Copyright, Designs and Patents Act of 1988. All rights reserved. No part of this book may be reproduced, or stored in a retrieval system, or transmitted in any form or by any means, electronic, mechanical, photocopying, recording, or otherwise, without the prior written permission of both the author and the above publisher of this book All imagery and illustrations

© Alan R. Massen

Neither the publisher nor the author can accept liability for the use of any of the materials, methods or information recommended in this book or for any consequences arising out of their use, nor can they be held responsible for any errors or omissions that may be found in the text or may occur at a future date as a result of changes in rules, laws or equipment All manufacturers, sellers, product names and services identified in this book are used in editorial fashion and for the benefit of such companies with no intention of any infringement of trademarks. No such use or the use of any trade name is intended to convey endorsement or other affiliation with this book. Every effort has been made to obtain the necessary permissions with reference to copyright material, both illustrative and quoted. We apologize for any omissions in this respect and will be pleased to make the appropriate acknowledgements in any future edition.

Paperback Edition ISBN 978-0-9935591-3-6
Typeset in Minion Pro

Published in Great Britain by Rainbow Publications UK

About the Author

Alan was born in the city of Norwich in the county of Norfolk, England in November 1949. When Alan was still a teenager he started painting whilst attending art classes in Norwich. In his mid-teens he had two paintings accepted for a National Art Exhibition held in London and other major UK cities. Alan spent most of his working life as a professional Health and Safety Advisor and rarely picked up a paint brush until Alan, his wife Susie and daughter Ginny (his other daughter Mandy is married and lives with her husband Adrian in Sheffield) moved out of the city of Norwich into the countryside in 1993. They moved to a little village called East Lexham in the heart of Norfolk. The village was very peaceful and pretty. This helped inspire Alan to take up watercolour painting once again. In 2004 they moved to another small West Norfolk village near Downham Market where they still live today. In 2008 Alan had to retire due to ill health (bad knees) and whilst he still painted regularly he began to spend more and more time gardening. In 2013 his wife Susie suggested that he kept a gardening diary to record his adventures in the garden and capture the changing seasons, animals, birds and the successes and failures of being a gardener he encountered. By the following year Susie suggested that he should write a book from his diary and include illustrations of both the garden and his artwork. In 2014 Alan's first book was published by Creative Gateway called **"Retiring to the Garden – Year One".** This proved such a success that Alan decided to follow this up with his second book called **"Retiring into a Rainbow"** featuring his watercolour paintings. He then in 2015 published **"Retiring to Our Garden – Year Two"** published this time by Rainbow Publications UK. He then re-issued his first two books this time in a **"Second Edition"**. Also published by Rainbow Publications UK. In 2016 he published: **"Skiathos a Greek Island Paradise", "Norfolk the County of my Birth", "Art Inspired by a Rainbow", "Ibiza Island of Dreams", "Majorca Island in the Sun", "Flip-flops and Shades on Thassos", "Mardle and a Troshin' in Norfolk", "England the Country of my Birth", "Mousehole the Cornish Jewel", "Sunshine and Shades on Kefalonia", and finally "Shades and Flip-flops on Zakynthos"** Also published by Rainbow Publications UK. He has recently started on the following new books which will be entitled: **"Crete and the Island of Santorini", "Cyprus the Pyramids and the Holy Land", "Corfu and Mainland Greece", "Trips into my Mind's Eye", "Flip-flops and Shades on many Greek Islands"** and finally **"Greece Land of Gods and Men".** In 2020 he produced this book which is a 3rd edition of **"Mardle and a Troshin' in Norfolk"** also published by Rainbow Publications UK.

Alan…

I hope you will enjoy mardling and a Troshin with me…

Books by Alan R. Massen

Retiring to the Garden Year 1 - Paperback
Retiring into a Rainbow - Paperback and Hardback
Retiring into a Rainbow - 1st Edition - My Favourite Artwork 2020 - 1st Edition
Retiring to our Garden Year one - 1st & 2nd Editions
Retiring to our Garden Year two - 1st & 2nd & 3rd Editions
Retiring into a Rainbow - 1st & 2nd Editions
Skiathos a Greek Island Paradise - 1st & 2nd & 3rd Editions
Norfolk the County of my Birth - 1st & 2nd & 3rd Editions
Art Inspired by a Rainbow - 1st & 2nd & 3rd & 4th Editions
Ibiza Island of Dreams - 1st & 2nd Editions
Majorca Island in the Sun - 1st & 2nd Editions
Flip-Flops and Shades on Thassos - 1st & 2nd & 3rd Editions
Mardle and a Troshin' in Norfolk - 1st & 2nd & 3rd Editions
England the Country of my Birth - 1st & 2nd Editions
Mousehole the Cornish Jewel - 1st & 2nd & 3rd Editions
Sunshades & Flip-Flops on Kefalonia - 1st & 2nd & 3rd Editions
Shades & Flip-Flops on Zakynthos - 1st & 2nd & 3rd Editions
Trips into my Minds Eye - 1st & 2nd & 3rd & 4th Editions
Corfu and Mainland Greece - 1st & 2nd & 3rd Editions
Crete and the Island of Santorini - 1st & 2nd & 3rd Editions
Cyprus - Pyramids - Holy Land - 1st & 2nd & 3rd Editions
Greek Islands in the Sun - 1st & 2nd & 3rd Editions
Being Greek - 1st & 2nd & 3rd Editions

E-books and Booklets by Alan R. Massen:

Retiring to the Garden Yr 1 - Retiring into a Rainbow - My Art 1997 - 2018 - Skiathos a Greek Paradise Island
My Norfolk - My Greece - My England - My Team - My Skiathos - My Art - My Album of Visual Art
My Village - Greece Land of Gods and Men - Norfolk Wildlife - Civilisation (Empires of the Past)
Boudica Queen of the Iceni - Roman Britain

Susie and Alan…

Copyright © 2020 - Alan R. Massen
Published in Great Britain by Rainbow Publications UK.

Dedication

Welcome and this book that features ten months in my life as we go a **"Mardle and a Troshin' in Norfolk"**. I would like to dedicate this publication to all the people of Norfolk especially my aunty Joyce, Beryl, Phyllis, Dennis and my late uncle Frank, son Paul, my Mum and Dad who all in their time spoke my kind of language. I would also like to thank my surgeon Mr. James Jeffery FRCS, our friends Andy, Lynn, Karl, Anna, Alistair, Issy, Mandy, Ginny, Ann, Lou, Gerard, Olivia and my wife Susie and our dogs Poppy and Charlie for putting up with me on our many journeys together mardling and a troshin' around Norfolk and beyond.

To all of our family, friends and you my reader I hope that you will enjoy this my latest book…

Contents

Introduction ………………..………………………	1
July 2015 …………….. ……………………………	8
August 2015…………… ………………………..	22
September 2015 …..…………………………..	41
October 2015 ……………………………………..	53
November 2015 ..………………………………..	76
December 2015 ……..…..………………………	88
January 2016 …. ………….…..…………………	95
February 2016 …………………………….…..…	101
March 2016 …………………………………….…	107
April 2016 …………………………………….…..	115
Mardling and a Troshin' to the End ……………..	122
My 2020 Artworks	137
Acknowledgement ……………………………..	212

Copyright © 2020 Alan R. Massen

Introduction

Featured below is Alan enjoying the Norfolk sunshine, a fishing boat high and dry at Cromer and a view of Blakeney harbour.

Welcome to my book which is called **"Mardle and a Troshin' in Norfolk"** and as the title suggests it's an old Norfolk boy's ramblings (me) on a journey through ten months of my everyday life experiences of living in the county of my birth. Although we will start by learning something about the Norfolk dialect. I will however, not be using the dialect very much in the main chapters of this book as I realise that nobody outside of Norfolk would have a clue what it meant. For example: hold you hard and co to heck it's a rum load of old Squit! See what I mean! The last sentence means: wait a moment he exclaimed and what a load of old nonsense…

Introduction

Old Father Time…

Norfolk Wildlife…

This year (2020) I have reach the age of seventy plus years of age! I have begun to realise that much of my life is now behind me and that I am now beginning the inevitable downhill phase of my life towards the great adventure! Since becoming an old person, I have noticed that every day, month and year goes by much quicker than it did before and most people that I meet are now much younger than myself. This realisation has helped me to focus on the here and now. I try everyday to treasure and enjoy every moment, everything around me and smile as much as I can. To help me do this I have recently (4 years now) stopped smoking after more than fifty years, started walking the dogs most days and started a diet to reduce my current overweight self-down to something much healthier. I live in hope!…

Introduction

Wells Next The Sea Norfolk beach huts

Whilst I enjoy reflecting on the fond memories of the past and the people that I have known I believe that you should always look to the future. It is not always healthy to spend too much time reflecting and remembering the past although it is important not to forget your past. So to help me to stop looking back to much I started in 2015 to not only trying to enjoy every new day as much as I could but also to write down any key personal events and experiences I had as they happened. So after just ten months I had a significant number of diary entries of everyday events written down. So as I have done in some of my other books that I have written in the past I set about writing this book. I hope you will enjoy joining me in this personal journey of ten months in my life. The artwork in this book has been produced by either scanning photographs or my watercolour paintings into my computer and then using a piece of art software on my PC that gives them an Impressionist effect…a bit like Claude Monet. Before we set off I thought the non-Norfolk reader may enjoy some brief examples of the strange way Norfolk folk speak and a few of the peculiar words we use. The Norfolk dialect is not heard so often these days but it can still be heard in the Norfolk countryside and villages. So after you have experienced and marvelled at our rich heritage of Norfolk dialect and the way we communicate in Norfolk, as I have already mentioned, I will not be using any of these words or expressions within the main body of my book however, my Norfolk roots may, however, inadvertently express themselves in the grammar that I use…

Introduction

Alan in the Norfolk sun…

Examples of the Norfolk way of speaking

ar ya reet bor? - (are you all right neighbour)

bred and born - (used instead of "born and bred")

co ter heck – (an exclamation of amazement)

come on ter rain – (starts to rain)

cor blarst me – (oh blast me)

dew yew keep a Troshin – (goodbye and take care)

directly – (as soon as or immediately)

fare y'well – (goodbye)

fumble fisted – (clumsy)

good on'yer – (good for you or good of you)

he'll square yew up – (he will chastise you)

he dint ortera dun it – (he ought not to have done it)

Introduction

High and Dry in Norfolk…

More examples of the Norfolk way of speaking

hold you hard – (hang on or wait a moment)

lolloping along – (strolling along)

mind how you go – (good-bye)

my heart alive! – (expression of surprise)

on the huh – (not level)

putting on his/her parts (a tantrum or acting up)

slummocking great mawther – (fat girl)

thas a rummun – (it's very strange)

that'll larn yer – (that will teach you)

tergether – (greeting people/couples walking)

wus up? – (what is wrong)

yesterdi – (yesterday)

Introduction

The Norfolk Broads…

Now we have explored some of the strange ways the people of Norfolk speak we will now enjoy some of the strange individual words, and there meaning, used as part of the everyday Norfolk dialect:

Barney – An argument

Bishy, bishy barney bee – Ladybird

Bor – Neighbour or boy

Chimley – Chimney

Claggy – Muddy or moist

Dudder – To shiver or shake

Dwile – Floor cloth

Friz – Frozen

Hull – To throw

Loke – Narrow lane or unmade-up road

Introduction

Beach huts at Wells…

Some more Norfolk dialect words

Mawther – Girl

Mardle – To gossip, chat or talk

Mob – To scold or nag

Queer – Out of sorts or ill

Rum – Queer or odd

Squit – Load of old nonsense

Troshin' – Threshing or to go for a long walk

Having spent some time exploring the way the people of Norfolk speak and looking at some of the words we use which all help makes up the distinct Norfolk dialect we will leave this strange language behind and enter into an old Norfolk boy's ramblings on ten months in his life:

So let's all go a Mardle and a Troshin' in Norfolk together…

July 2015

Susie settling down with our dogs Poppy and Charlie

Our dogs Charlie and Poppy are now over a year old (born 24.06.14.) and have been with us since the 24th August 2014. They have settling down well. Susie takes them out for a long walk whenever she can to the forestry commissions wood, that is not too far from where we live. When my right knee is not to painful (I am waiting for a total right knee replacement operation) and I have managed to get a reasonable amount of sleep, I will go with them. I had an operation to replace my left knee last April and thankfully it is well on the way to a full recovery. Our dogs are a brother and sister act and spend much of their day playing on our back garden lawn, weather permitting. The puppies are very different from each other in looks and colouring that it is amazing that they are related let alone brother and sister. Charlie has a black coat and Poppy has a white and black coat. It gives us hours of pleasure watching them charging around playing. It is really amazing, seeing them develop and grow into well balanced companions for each other and for us. We are so pleased that we decided, last year, to get this brother and sister act to come and share our life together. **Update 2020:** Our dogs have grown up to be wonderful companions for us and each other. We walk them everyday in our local woods. My right knee has also now been replaced. Both my replacement knee joints are not altogether great but they are much better then they were before my surgery! …

July 2015

The Queen Elizabeth II Hospital in Kings Lynn

Leaving the crutches behind: It has now been three months since I had a total left knee replacement operation at the Queen Elizabeth Hospital in Kings Lynn and my recovery from the surgery continues to improve day by day. My improvement is largely down to the skills of my orthopaedic specialist surgeon Mr. James Jeffery and his surgical team. Initially my recovery was slow and my wound was slow to heal but with good care and physiotherapy my knee slowly began to respond and my pain began to ease. At the beginning of July I was able to discard the pair of elbow crutches the hospital had loaned me and walk unaided. This meant that I could now come up and down the stairs without the need for the support that they gave. I have also been able to stop taking my strong pain control medication as I am now largely pain free however, I am not totally pain free, as my right knee is painful, from time to time, and will require the same operation as my left knee had real soon. My improved mobility means that after six months of frustration at not being able to do any gardening or to help Susie with other everyday tasks I can now do some light lifting, plant watering, flower dead heading and other small tasks inside and out. As I get stronger and more mobile I hope to be able to do more and more. **Update 2020:** In December 2018 and again in December 2019 I returned to see my surgeon because both replacement knee joints, after x-rays, were still causing me some discomfort. He said both times that my left knee replacement showed signs of bone thinning and may need another knee replacement operation sometime in the future. My right knee replacement joint appeared more stable at the moment. He will now see me on a regular basis to review this to ensure that my knees have not yet reached the stage where further surgery is required to replace either one!…

July 2015

Andrew and Lynn at Troulos Bay on Skiathos in 2018 and their dog Franky who sadly died in February 2020

Rango Tango Hip Operation: Our good friend Andrew went into his local Sheffield hospital earlier this month to have a right hip replacement operation. I am pleased to say the surgery was successful and he has now made a full recovery. So like me he now has brand new surgical equipment inside him. We first met our friend Andrew (Rango Tango) and his wife Lynn on holiday, at the Troulos Bay Hotel, on Skiathos, some years ago and have been good friends ever since. Andrew was given his nickname from his holiday beach tennis partner Dori (who doubles up as the hotel pool and beach attendant as well as gardener). Dori said it was the way that Andrew moves when playing tennis that suggested the name Rango Tango. Andrew, following his recovery from his operation, and Lynn will be coming to stay with us for a few days later this year and we are very much looking forward to seeing them and their happy dog Franky. We also plan to visit them at their house near Sheffield in October during our holiday to Edale in Derbyshire. **Update 2020:** Since his operation in 2015 Andy, I am pleased to say, has made a full recovery unfortunately he also has had to have surgery in 2018 to remove a cancerous growth which also I am happy to report was successful. So lets hope that he continues to be well from now on. Lynn and Andy, I am please to say, went back to Troulos Bay Hotel on Skiathos last year and are planning to go again this year for there summer holiday. I am sure that they will have a great time however, sadly they lost their lovely dog Franky recently!…

July 2015

 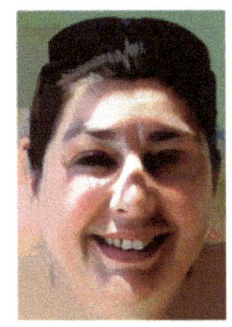 

Keeping up the good work

Because of my operation over the last few months Susie has not only had to continue working full time but has had to also nurse me, walk the dogs, keep the house clean and tidy, cook all our meals and take over all of the many gardening tasks that I could not do because of my recent surgery. She has really done a great job and the flowers that she planted in our garden, this year, are looking spectacular. Susie has also kept up the good work by mowing the lawn, watering the many flower pots, flower beds and also feeding the plants, as and when required. As well as all this she has found the time to redesign the layout and planting in our greenhouse. Susie has done all of the above without any complaint and in fact has, I think, enjoyed showing me how it should be done judging by the happy smile that she always seems to have on her face. **Update 2020:** Susie currently now works two days a week. She has done this since August 2019. It has been great for me and the dogs to have her at home most days, however, she moved up to two days a week due to work commitments. As my knees now cause me far less pain then before my knee replacements we now tend to do the gardening together, however, Susie still undertakes the more heavy lifting task as my knees are still not great and I have to be careful!

Poppy and Charlie's first holiday

Susie and I decided this month that as my left knee has healed up so well it was time to reward ourselves and the dogs with a change of scenery. This will be the first holiday that we have all been away together (us and the dogs). Susie suggested that we book a cottage in Derbyshire so we could not only take the dogs out walking in the dales but also visit family and friends who all live in and around the Sheffield area. Obviously we had to find somewhere that allowed you to take two dogs so we spent a morning looking at cottage rental sites on the Internet. We also decided to go at the end of October so that we would be there when Susie's sister Lou's daughter Olivia would be on holiday from school. **Update 2020:** I am sad to say that since going to Derbyshire in 2015, due to poorly knees, we have not been away from our Norfolk home on holiday but, maybe we will be able to this year!…

July 2015

Holiday plan: Edale in Derbyshire

After many hours of doing our research we decided to book a cottage in Edale in Derbyshire for a week in October 2015. Edale is a small village at the start and or end of the UK's first and most famous long distance walking path (depending on where you start from) called the Pennine Way. The village itself grew from the herdsmen's shelters or booths that are now the hamlets of Upper Booth, Barber Booth, Ollerbrook Booth and Nether Booth. The central booth was Grindsbrook Booth which is now usually called Edale Village. The village has two popular pubs, a cafe and a local shop. The village also has a railway station on one of England's most spectacular railway routes: the Manchester to Sheffield train line. The village of Edale is pretty and lies on a side road off the main road along the valley. There is a large car-park at the road junction and the railway station is just nearby. Just above it is The Rambler, the first of the two pubs in the village. The road into the village proper continues past Fieldhead, the Peak National Park's information centre and camp site, past the church and on to end at a small square outside the school and the second of the villages pubs called the Old Nag's Head. The village of Edale is usually accepted as the start of the Pennine Way. Just opposite lies the Post Office and general store and Cooper's Farm camp site which is an alternative to the National Park Site up at the top of the village near the train station. At the head of the valley, in Barber Booth, it is often possible to obtain teas at weekends and there are several campsites between here and Edale village. Further down the valley, horse rides are available at Lady Booth Farm in Nether Booth. There is a Youth Hostel high on the side of Kinder at Rowland Cote, above Nether Booth…

July 2015

The Old Dairy cottage in Barber Booth in Edale

Having made our choice of where to go we then needed to find and book somewhere to stay. We picked the Old Dairy in Barber Booth and booked it for a week. We booked this cottage because we are able to take our two dogs. This attractive, detached, former dairy with its pretty courtyard and a wealth of original beams and exposed stone walls is set in the peaceful little hamlet of Barber Booth. There are excellent walks from the doorstep whilst being within a couple of miles from the picturesque village of Edale and the start of the Pennine Way. So come October we will all be off to spend our first holiday away with our dogs…

July 2015

My book

Knee review up-date: In early July I decided to make an appointment with my Doctor to review my still troublesome right knee which I had injured stepping out of the greenhouse in May 2014. I also wanted to review my medication and give him a copy of my latest book **"Retiring into a Rainbow"**. When I went to my appointment with Dr. Phillip Koopowitz we decided that he would refer me back to see Mr. James Jeffery for him to give us his expert opinion as to what was wrong with my right knee. He also discontinued my current strong pain killing tablets and replaced these with a general lower strength pain killer, just in case I needed them. The Doctor was delighted to be given a copy of my new book, as this features many of my paintings. After he had a look inside the book, he said he liked many of them, and as his wife is also an artist, he said he was looking forward to taking the book home and sharing it with her. **Update 2020:** I am sad to report that, even after five years, my left knee replacement joint is still causing me pain issues. I have been back to my GP and surgeon on several occassions over this period and have recently had to go back onto the strong pain killing tablets. This is sad and the specialist said when I saw him in December 2019 that I may have to undergo knee replacement surgery again on this knee as the surrounding bone is showing signs of thinning and wearing down. He said he will see me again next year and then every year thereafter for new x-rays and examinations to see if the wear and tear has reached the stage where further surgical intervention is required…

July 2015

The College of West Anglia

Work life balance

During my knee surgery recuperation in April 2015 Susie and I spent some time talking about her work life balance, as we had noticed, in recent months, that her job had become more intense and her job stresses had increased considerably, which meant that she did not enjoy her job very much anymore. We did a review of our financial commitments and came to the joint conclusion that we could just about manage financially and that Susie would give three month's notice to the College of West Anglia (seen above) where she works and leave on the 20th July. She will then have a few months rest before finding a part time job come the New Year. Susie expressed the wish to finish the current projects she is working on, which ends this October. As a valued employee the college asked Susie to do just that by returning, after a two weeks break, for two months part time (Wednesday and Thursday mornings) before finally leaving the college in early October. Therefore, by mid-July Susie was on holiday before returning back to work, part time, briefly, before *"retiring"* for a few months. We are all looking forward to her being at home with us more often that is to say the dogs and me. **Update 2020:** I am glad to report that Susie has been working first just one day a week since 2015 and then two days since 2019 and even better she is still working for the College of West Anglia. Her work life balance has improved dramatically in the last five years and today Susie is far more relaxed, healthy and enjoying her extra time at home with the dogs, the garden and me!…

July 2015

Taking cuttings…

Butterfly Heaven…

Making new life

One of the joys of being a gardener, at this time of year, is that you get the chance of making new life. For many plants this is achieved by taking cuttings of current plants and propagating them into healthy and strong new plants (and best of all they are also free) so you can increase your flower stocks for next year. In mid-July Susie and I took thirty cuttings of some of our current garden flowers which included Fuchsia, Salvia, Penstemon, Daisy and Myrtle. By using my rooting "Magic Powder" (hormone powder) and one litre pots filled with compost, we carefully placed each separate cutting into its own pot before giving it a good watering and putting them into our propagation frame. All we need to do now is keep an eye on them, water when necessary and sit back and watch the new life grow. **Update 2020:** I am please to report that every year since 2015 we have continued to take cuttings of our favourite plants, raise seeds and grow our own tomatoes in our greenhouse. Our garden is now a testament to the success we have had from doing this. This year we have successfully over-wintered about eighty cuttings in our greenhouse and we hope to raised even more new life this spring and summer from seeds and more plant cuttings. We are well pleased with our efforts so far in our garden and what is even better its all FREE…

July 2015

A squirrel feeding on our garden lawn and a field of Norfolk poppies

A hop, skip and a jump

On the first day of Susie's holiday from working (21st July) she took our two dogs for a walk in the woods while I stayed at home, and had a cup of tea on the patio in the summer sun, as my right knee was very painful that day. While I sat on the patio enjoying the sunny and warm morning, out of the corner of my eye I spotted a squirrel hoping and skipping across our back lawn and jumping up into our silver birch tree. Quickly he made his way up the tree and onto the peanut feeder and started to feed. A short time later another squirrel came hopping and skipping across the lawn. The first squirrel immediately came down the tree and chased the newcomer away before returning to his feeding. After about an hour Susie returned with the dogs and the squirrel was off like a shot. **Update 2020:** I am sorry to say that in recent years the squirrels have been notable by their absence I think due to our dogs running around barking, however, who knows they may be back again real soon. We can but live in hope!…

July 2015

A kingfisher with his tea and a Foxy Tale!

When Susie came into the back garden after returning with the dogs from their walk she joined me on the patio and I told her about the squirrel coming to feed (it comes most days when the dogs are out) and also about the second one that was chased off by the first. After listening to my story patiently Susie then told me that her walk with the dogs had also been eventful. Walking down one of the wide paths through the woods she noticed two foxes sitting in the sun, some hundred yards further down the path. The dogs spotted them and went charging down the path barking. This was all too much for the foxes and they were off like a flash. She went on to tell me that she often see rabbits, deer, woodpeckers, kingfishers and other birds when she takes the dogs into the local woods. I will be glad when my knee gets better and I can join them once again on these adventures. **Update 2020:** I am pleased to say that both Susie and I continue to walk our dogs daily and we see lots of Norfolk wildlife like owls, kingfishers, badgers, foxes, deer, hares and rabbits, to name but a few, on most days either in the nearby woods or when we drive down to one of the North Norfolk beaches that are close by!…

July 2015

Storm over a field of straw in Norfolk

Any, Any Old Iron - My Vauxhall Zafira

On the 24th July it was time to take my car for its annual M.O.T. at Thurlow Nunn in Kings Lynn. I have taken it to that same garage, where I purchased it from, for the last seven years and it has always passed the test first time, every time. Because I have had problems with my left knee for many years, we decided, years ago, that it would be a good idea, if I had a Vauxhall Zafira automatic because then I would not need to use my left leg and knee when driving. This has proved to be a great idea and has allowed me to continue to drive myself even with my disability. Now that I have a brand new total left knee replacement I was hopeful that my car would pass the M.O.T. again this time and I could continue driving once more. The good news is that it passed first time again, so after paying the test fee and collecting my car I returned home to give Susie the good news. **Update 2020:** I am sad to say that I no longer have the car featured above. It became the victim to being part of our cost cutting plans to save money. We moved onto only having one family car and used the money saved as part of our plan to help make up the shortfall in earnings that Susie would get when she moved from full time to part time working. But I still remember, my car, with great fondness and gratitude for all of its long, reliable and faithful service that it gave me !…

July 2015

My
Bleeding
Heart…

New Use for an old Wheelbarrow

Now that Susie is at home, on holiday, at the moment she has thrown herself into gardening. First she levelled and grass seeded parts of the back lawn that the dogs had worn out with all their running around. Next she used the hedge trimmer to cut back the honeysuckle that grows around the fence hiding our heating oil tank in our back garden. Following all this she emptied out our old wheelbarrow, in the front garden, that we use as a flower display container. She took the old plants and compost out before re-filling the wheelbarrow with fresh compost. We then went to Downham Home and Garden centre to get seven new alpine plants that she planted into her pre-papered "Old Wheelbarrow" when we got home. Watching her do all of this work really tired me out. **Update 2020:** I am please to say that Susie is still spending a lot of her time gardening. I emptied and re-composted the old wheelbarrow (06.03.2019) ready for us to buy new plants for it in the next few weeks. I will then watch Susie plant it up ready for it to have yet another colourful summer flower display in again this year!…

July 2015

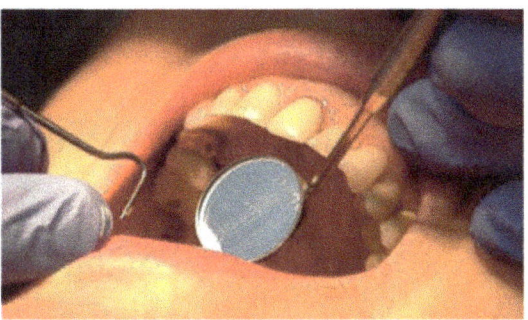

A Great Swelling of the Cheeks

On the 28th July, I woke up to find that my left cheek had swollen up like a football and was very painful. So at 9 am I phoned my dentists at Downham Market Dental Care Group. Luckily for me the receptionist was able to give me an appointment with my dentist Theo at 10.30 am that same day which was great. Having made my way to the surgery Theo sat me down in his dental chair and took a look inside my mouth. He said that I had an infection in my gum and that he would give me some medication to resolve this. He went on to tell me that my teeth however, were fine but needed a clean which I arrange for September before returning home via the chemists to get my medication. **Update 2020:** I am please to report that although I have been back to my dentist, every eight months for check-ups, over the last five years, I have had no further problem with my gums and neither have I had to have any other type of dental work done so all is well with my teeth so far but this may not be the case for much longer!…

August 2015

Sunset on the Norfolk coast…

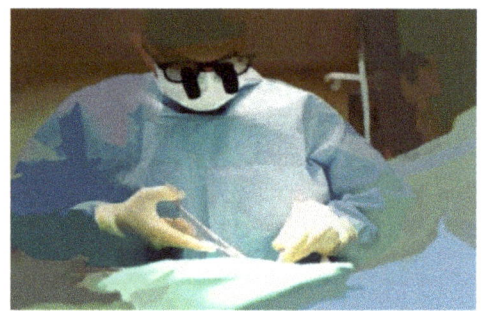

I'm Off to See the Wizard

Above is the wizard, well not really a wizard (although he is with his scalpel), he is an orthopaedic specialist surgeon. On the 1st August I received my hospital appointment with my orthopaedic specialist surgeon Mr. James Jeffery for the 11th September at 9 am. The appointment will be at the Queen Elizabeth hospital in Kings Lynn. Mr. Jeffery was the surgeon who operated on my left knee and now my doctor and I want his expert opinion on what is causing me the severe pain that I an getting, from time to time, in my right knee. It has been a problem and getting worse for the last sixteen months. My Doctor feels that it is caused by a ligament problem but I am not so sure so we agreed that I would get a second opinion from an expert. Hence the appointment. **Update 2020:** I am sad to say that since I wrote about the problems I was experiencing with my right knee things have moved on. In April 2016 where I underwent a partial right knee replacement operation. Again performed by Mr. Jeffery. I have since recovered however, I am still experiencing pain mostly in my left full knee replacement but also with the more recent right partial knee replacement. I recently went to see my surgeon in December 2018 and again in December 2019. He said that my left knee replacement showed signs of bone thinning and may need another knee replacement operation sometime in the future. My right knee replacement joint appeared more stable at the moment. He will continue to see me on a regular basis in the future until further surgery is required to replace them again. Watch this space!…

August 2015

Sowing the Seed

To celebrate being on holiday Susie decided to fence off the areas on the lawn that the dogs have damaged either by digging or just by charging around. She then levelled the lumps and bumps off before mixing grass seed with an equal amount of compost and then applying this mix to the pre-prepared areas. Her final act was to firm these seeded areas before watering the treated grass seeded areas. We will need to keep the new seed moist for the next seven days to help germination. Now it was just a matter of sitting back and waiting and watching the new grass grow. **Update 2020:** I am please to say that the grass did grow back and our lawn, touch wood, has stayed almost intact ever since!

Creating (more) New Life

Last month we took some cuttings of plants that we wanted to propagate ready for putting into the garden beds and pots next year. On the 2nd August we decided to increase the number of cuttings we had taken from twenty four up to forty. We filled, another sixteen one litre pots with compost and then I went around our garden beds and pots in search of suitable candidates from which to take further cuttings. Having made my selection I removed sections of un-flowering three inch cuttings from each plant, removed the bottom set of leaf buds and dipped each cutting into hormone powder before placing them individually into pots. This done it was time to wait for nature to take its course! **Update 2020:** I am please to say that every year since we have repeated this task so that most of the plants that we now have in our garden have been created by us for free. This is a great way to fill up your garden and pots with wonderful colour for very little expense!…

August 2015

Finding the stepping stones

We have had to step through the muddy area leading from the gravel up onto the lawn (see above) for the last year as our dogs have managed to create an area of worn out grass about 50 cm wide and 4 m long that leads directly from the gravel at our back kitchen door onto the lawn proper. When Susie levelled, fenced off and re-seeded the lawn in two areas near our silver birch tree she left un-seeded the worn area mentioned above. As we waited for the new sown grass seed to grow we discussed how we could resolve this final issue. As it would be difficult to fence off this worn out area because it is the only viable access onto the main area of lawn we decided that we would sink eight 40 cm round stepping stones into the worn area and then seed around them. This would allow the dogs and people to access the main lawn by using the stepping stones thus allowing the seed to germinate. We thought that this offered the best solution and would hopefully be a permanent one. So on the 2nd August, after completing our potting up of cuttings we set off to visit Downham Home and Garden Centre to see if we could find eight suitable stepping stones…

August 2015

Selecting and Placing the Stepping Stones

The garden centre had a good selection of stepping stones and after spending some time considering the merits of various designs. We settled on eight 40 cm round stepping stones that were made out of concrete and modelled to look like 5 cm slices of tree trunk. So along with a bag of sharpe sand we loaded them onto a trolley, went and paid for them before loading them into the back of my car and took them home. After a coffee break (you should always find the time for a coffee), we offloaded our sand and stepping stones and took them into our back garden. Then it was time to get down to work. First we positioned each stone where we wanted it to go before drawing around it with a nail so we could see where each individual hole needed to go, to allow each stone to be sunk into the ground surface so it would be just below the level of the surrounding grass, when it is was put into place. Having done this we used an edging spade to dig around the eight marked out impressions and removed the soil down to 8 cm deep so we could put 3 cm of Sharpe sand into the bottom of each hole, level this off before placing each stepping stone into its allocated position.

Working like a Team

Working as a team, Susie and I spent about three hours marking out, digging out, introducing sharpe sand, levelling the sand, and then placing individual stepping stones into their allocated place, ensuring each stone was level and was just below the surrounding grass level. Having achieved what we thought was a good outcome and checking that the stepping stones had the right spacing between each stone Susie then seeded around each stone before we stepped back to admire our hard work. The picture above was taken a week later showing how much the grass seed had grown around the stepping stones in such a short time. We were well pleased.
Update 2020: I am sad to say that this was NOT the final solution, as we had hoped, to this problem. It worked to a certain extent but it still managed to get quite treacherous when wet or icy!. In 2020 we decided to bite the bullet and remove all of the turf from the right hand arbour up to the top of the left hand boarder and graveled it. This has worked very well and fingers crossed it will now drain away much more quickly and not get muddy again!…

August 2015

All Washed Up…

The oil tank being filled up…

Getting prepared for the Winter

I thought that even though we are only in August consideration needed to be given to the inevitable arrival of the cold winter months and so planning ahead was essential. Part of that planning is to check how much heating oil we have left in our storage tank. As the gauge told me that our tank was well below half full I decided to arrange for a top up from Goff Petroleum in the next few days. This they did a week later so we now have enough oil to last us through the winter months ahead. It was good to get this done so early as the heating oil prices are always a bit cheaper during the summer months and after all it was one less thing to worry about. **Update 2020:** I am sure, like many others, we have continued to make sure, every year since that we have a sufficient supply of heating oil in our tank to last us through the cold winter months!…

August 2015

The College of West Anglia in Kings Lynn

The Hero Returns

Susie, who has had the last two weeks at home, before returning back to the college on the 4th August. She will be on a temporary two month contract, at the College of West Anglia to complete the projects that she had been managing up to when she left her full time post in July. She will only be working a full day on a Wednesday and a half day on a Thursday for the next eight weeks, before once again retiring back to the dogs and me. This is unless the college management offer her a permanent part time position. As she works so hard, and is seen as something of a hero, by her senior managers, I think they will indeed offer her a position thus keeping a valued member of staff. I think Susie would be happy to stay and work part time at the college because she enjoys working with the people at the college very much.

The lone watering can in our greenhouse after Susie had returned to work

Update 2020: I am pleased to report, that unusually as it is, I was right and Susie was offered, by the management of the college, more part time work. In fact she is still there to this very day doing two days a week!…

August 2015

Then…

and

Now…

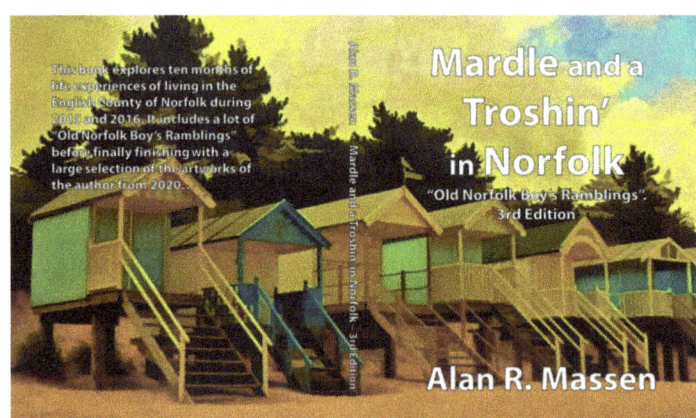

Another One Bites the Dust - Then and Now

n the 5th August, the weather was very wet so I stayed indoors and completed the first draft of my latest book called "Flip-flops and Shades on Thassos". This is the 12th book that I have had published and features the Greek Island of Thassos where we have had some very enjoyable family holidays in the past. In the book I used text and artwork pictures in an attempt to give my readers an insight into this lovely Greek holiday island. Not only have I included the history of the island but taken the reader on a journey around the island in words and pictures so they can see for themselves some of the beautiful scenery, places and golden beaches that await them should they decide to visit Thassos for themselves. **Update 2020:** I am very pleased to report, that in the last five years I have continued to write and have published more than forty five books. Today in March 2020 once again you will find me writing my latest book called: Mardle and a Troshin in Norfolk - 3rd Edition. They say something's never change!…

August 2015

A thrush on our green, green, grass of home

An otter in the rivers of Norfolk

The Green, Green, Grass of Home

By the 7th August the two fenced off areas on our lawn that Susie had levelled and grass seeded and also the stepping stone walkway that we had seeded had started to grow. August is obviously a good month to re-seed the lawn. It is great to see that all of our hard work is being rewarded. We will once again have a completely un-damaged lawn. This may not remain the case for very long however, as our dogs are likely to wear more patches or dig more holes in it again in the future. Now that we know how successful re-seeding of the lawn is we should be able to always maintain our green, green, grass of home. Well maybe!…

August 2015

We are Back in the Big Time Again - and - Again!

I have been supporting Norwich City Football Club for more than fifty years and I have seen many ups and downs over the years. However; this season is one of those great **UPS** that do not come along often enough for football supporters of our club. Last season Norwich City where promoted back to the Premier League after just one year in the Championship. On the 8th August it was time for the big kick off back in the big time. So the new season began and Norwich started their campaign by playing Crystal Palace at home. Although they lost 3 – 1 they played very well and where unlucky to lose so all may not be lost for the rest of the coming season. That is the joy of our national game you never know what will happen. **Update 2020:** I have first sad news and then great news and maybe more bad news to follow. First my club was relegated back down again in 2016 **BUT THEN** in 2019 great joy came again when: **We are the Champions again my Friend.** My football team Norwich City FC (the Canaries of Carrow Road, Norwich) who I have been supporting for more than sixty years. Made my dreams come true when on Sunday 5th May 2019 Norwich City beat Aston Villa 2 - 1 away to finish Champions of the Championship and gain promotion back to the Premier League next season. In November 2019 I was seventy years of age and I am so proud and excited that my team is playing, against the big boys, once more in the top division of the English football league. Not everything is good news however, as I write this book in March 2020 my team is propping up the rest and will probably get relegated once more in May 2020! Oh well never mind such is the ups and downs of life! On the Ball City - Come on you YELLOWS. **Latest Update 2020:** Yesterday Wednesday 4th March 2020 Norwich City beat Tottenham Hotspurs away to reach the last eight of the FA Cup. They will play Manchester United at home in the quarter finals ad then who know maybe, if we beat them, we will go to Wembley once AGAIN! We live in HOPE - ALWAYS. On the Ball City - Come on you YELLOWS…

August 2015

A wild rabbit in the field behind our house…

Poppy and Charlie…

Getting longer to rest and the BIG Bake Off!

Our dogs Poppy and Charlie, thankfully, are now regularly sleeping past 6 am. This is great, as before they were often awake much earlier. As Susie only has to be up early for work on a Wednesday and Thursday morning to go to work we find that now getting up a bit later is most welcome. I think the dogs are sleeping later because Susie is only working two days a week and the dogs are much more relaxed and getting into the swing of having her company much more often. Another reason why the dogs are not waking up so early is that Susie now takes the dogs out on long walks most days so they are getting a lot more exercise. I accompany her on these walks when the pain in my right knee permits. I also benefit, by Susie having more time at home, because she spends more time in the kitchen baking, using recipes from her extensive library of cookery books. An added bonus is that I get to enjoy sampling the lovely cakes, pastries and pies that she now bakes on a regular basis. **Update 2020:** I am pleased to report, that the dogs continue to sleep well but now they sleep until 7 am. This is also great for us because with Susie only currently working two days a week most days we get a lay in. As I sit here writing this book today (March 2020) Susie is once more in the kitchen baking. I wonder what delights we will be enjoying later on today!…

August 2015

The Final Draft

On the 12th August I finished working on the final draft of my 4th book which is called: **"Retiring to Our Garden – Year Two"**. The book features Susie and my gardening experiences and the joys of gardening in our Norfolk garden for the second year together. Roy Baldwin (who sadly died in November 2018) has kindly agreed to edit my latest book. Once completed my publisher will organise the printing and distribution of my latest offering.

Talking about publishers I have recently changed my publisher from **Creative Gateway** to **Rainbow Publications UK** and therefore, my latest book and those that follow will be published by my new publisher…

August 2015

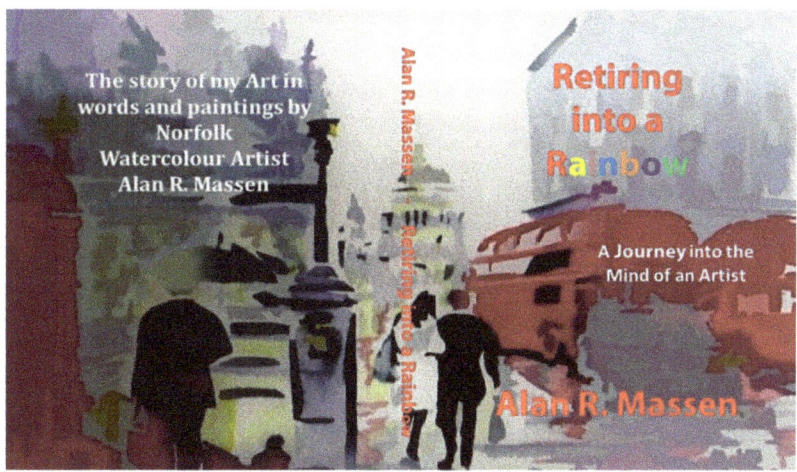

Getting the 2nd Editions Ready

On the 13th August, while I waited for Roy to complete the editing of my 4th book and before I produce the final edition ready to submit to my publisher I decided to update my first two books ready for re-publication. These will be my 5th and 6th books to be published now in **2nd Editions.** They are called **"Retiring to Our Garden – Year One"** and **"Retiring into a Rainbow"**. I worked on them all day and introduced new cover layouts, updated some of the illustrations and pictures and text in both books. My new publisher Rainbow Publications UK wants to re-issue these books immediately after the publication of my 4th book…

August 2015

Alan in a restaurant in the Old Port Skiathos Town and my Skiathos book cover

Back to my Keyboard

The weather in mid-August has been very poor with cloud, heavy rain and mainly Northerly winds. This has meant that I have had the time to spend indoors on my keyboard, working on the draft of my 7th book. This time I am writing the story in words and pictures of our many holidays to the paradise Greek island of Skiathos. Of all the Mediterranean island we have visited in the last twenty five years this one is our all time favourite. The book will therefore, be called **"Skiathos a Greek Island Paradise"**. I think it will take about two months to complete the draft ready for editing and then submitting it for publishing. I really enjoy spending time developing my story lines and producing artwork that reflect our love of and our experiences of holidaying on this truly beautiful paradise island. **Update 2020:** I am sad to say that Susie and I have not been back to Skiathos since our last holiday there in the summer of 2014. Sad but true. Maybe we will return again one day. Oh I do hope so!…

August 2015

The Simple Solution are Always the Best

Have you ever noticed that it is usually the simple solutions that are the best solutions to many a problem? We had a problem with small pieces of half eaten fat balls falling out of our bird fat ball feeder onto the lawn where the dogs would snaffle them up. Thinking that the fat balls would not do the dogs stomachs much good at all what we needed was a simple solution to stop this from happening. As the feeder was made of an enclosed wire mesh tube, with gaps to allow the birds to feed on the food, meant that when the food inside got smaller it could easily fall through these gaps in the bottom, and onto the lawn below. What to do? Then I remembered that I had a small green plastic flower pot saucer under a nearby pot. This I took and drilled four small holes in the bottom of it and then wired this to the feeder base. This has worked really well and the birds have also found my redesign to their liking. Now the tray collects the small pieces, stopping them falling to the lawn below and the birds can then eat those up in the tray instead of the dogs getting them below. So everyone's a winner except the dogs. **Update 2020:** I am pleased to report, that today in March 2020 the solution we found is still in place and much to the dogs annoyance still works!

Simple Solution Number Two!

While we are on the subject of simple solutions another example has sprung to mind. Recently we fitted a fly curtain to the outside of our back kitchen door. It basically is two strips of net hanging down from the top and fixed to the sides of the door frame by Velcro. These strips then meet in the middle and are held shut by several magnets fixed down the middle of each strip edge. These have been a great success at keeping the flies out. The dogs wasted no time in learning how to push their way through the strips to get in or out of the kitchen. This left just one problem. When we needed to carry anything heavy or large either into or out of the kitchen it was very difficult to get through the net curtain safely and without damaging it. What to do? Susie suggested that we use small lengths of ribbon as tie backs and fix each curtain, using these, to hooks put into the wall on either side of the door frame. This would allow us to leave the curtain fixed to the door frame; open the curtain in the middle and using the ribbon tie each piece to the hooks in the wall. This has worked really well. **Update 2020:** I am pleased to report, that today in March 2020 the solution we found then has been working really well for the last five years. We do of course replace the fly curtains when required…

August 2015

The Seed Collectors

In April this year Susie sowed some wild flower seeds into one of our back garden flower beds. These all came up and have been really beautiful. By mid-August most of the wild flowers had blossomed and produced seed pods of one sort or another. As we sat on our patio having a coffee (you should always find time for a cup of coffee), one morning, we decided that we would enlarge an area in one of our flower beds in the autumn so we could have more wild flowers next year. With this in mind we started to collect any ripe wild flower seeds from our garden and stored them in brown paper envelopes in a kitchen cupboard ready for sowing early next spring. We will continue to collect ripe seed for the rest of this summer so not only will we have these lovely wild flowers once again next year but even better they will be completely **FREE. Update 2020:** I am pleased to say that we have continue the collection of seed from all of our garden plants, as well as taking numerous cutting every year since we stated doing this in 2015. Now in 2020 we have a significant collection of new young plants and packets of seeds that we will use again in this and future years. We must have save a fortune by now!

When the Red, Red, Robin Comes Bob, Bob, Bobbing Along!

One of the few sad things about being in our garden in the summer is that the robin, which had been in our garden over the autumn and winter, has been missing from our garden for the last few months. He has been off breeding and feeding in the fields and woods that surround our small Norfolk village. Imagine then our joy when on the 14th August he reappeared back in our garden on his favourite perch in the silver birch tree once again. He will stay with us now for the next eight months or so and be a constant companion when we are out in the garden digging or just enjoying the sunshine. When we are either sitting, pruning or digging outside the red, red robin will come bob, bob, bobbing along to see if we have turn up any nice big juicy garden worms for his tea!…

August 2015

Now it's Cuba Libre Time!

One of the great things about sitting in your garden on a warm summer's day is that a nice cold drink always goes down really well. My favourite cold drink is a tall glass of Cuba Libre. This consists of a squeezed whole lime, a large measure of Bacardi rum, lots of ice and a can of Pepsi. This combination makes the original cocktail of Cuban freedom. The drink was born when people were out celebrating Cuba's independence from Spain with a Bacardi, cola and lime an American soldier toasted "Por Cuba Libre" and the iconic name of the cocktail was born. **CHEERS! Update 2020:** I am very pleased to report, that today on the 8th March 2020 I will be having, as I have almost everyday since 2015, a couple of Cuba Libre's after I have finished my book writing for the day!

One Good Turn Deserves Another!

People say that one good turn deserves another and for me this month, this has proved to be correct. In early August, as Susie and I arrived in the car park to do our shopping at Tesco's in Downham Market when I noticed that someone had left their bag of shopping, purse, newspaper and other items in the trolley that we were about to use for our weekly shopping. Nobody was nearby so we waited a few minutes to see if anyone came to claim the bag and as nobody did we took it into the store and handed it in to the reception desk. The receptionist promised to try and identify the owner from the items in the bag. If this failed maybe, the owner would phone or maybe someone would come into the store to claim it. Hopefully this good deed has seen the return of these items to there rightful owner. I thought no more about it until the 18th August when I took my car to Kwik Fit to get them to investigate my near side rear tyre that had developed a slow puncture. After removing the tyre and examining it for punctures the fitter told me that the tyre was fine and the problem was that the valve was faulty. He then replaced this for me and thereby, fixed my problem. When I asked him how much the new valve was he said **"No charge"**. This obviously made me very happy indeed. then I remembered that I had done someone a good turn (the bag) and now I had been reward by someone else doing me a good turn. It proves what people say that what goes around comes around. **Update 2020:** I am very pleased to say, that I have continued to try to help others wherever possible over the last five years and I have also had favours done to me quite often from other people!…

August 2015

New Solar Lights for our Garden

When we went to visit our daughter Ginny recently, we noticed that she had several new solar lights in her garden. This inspired us to add to our own solar garden lights collection. When we got home we looked on the Internet and decided to get a patterned round pottery light, a blue pear shaped string of lights and for inside the kitchen a string of rose design lights. The later are battery powered with the others being solar powered. The round light we placed on the table on the patio and the pear shaped string of lights Susie fixed above the arch that leads from our back kitchen door car port into the rear garden. We left the solar lights switched off for two days to fully charge them up and when we switched them on two days later they all worked and looked great. **Update 2020:** I am very pleased to say, that most but not all of the solar lights mentioned above are still working today (Sunday 8th March 2020) however, some have failed and been thrown away whilst we have added others so this year we have more than 20 different solar lights some on the outside of our shed, some on the inside of our greenhouse, some on our outside house wall but the majority are in our garden borders. So there is much illumination by a host of solar lights in the garden!…

August 2015

Letting Susie Loose with the Strimmer

In June Susie seeded two worn areas of lawn with grass seed. Later in early August we grass seeded around some stepping stones that we had sunk into the lawn. By the 24th August all of the above seed had germinated and grown well, in fact it now required cutting. Since my recent knee surgery Susie has mown the lawn, whenever it has needed it, but we felt that the new grassed areas, would not stand up to being mowed by the heavy mower very well. I remembered that we had a grass strimmer in the shed that we had got to do our front grass bank last year. So getting it out of the shed, charging its battery up, Susie set about reducing the height of the new grass. This she did very well and now our lawn is looking complete once again. **Update 2020:** I am pleased to say, that the strimmer has now almost been made redundant! As I have already mentioned in February 2019 we replaced some of our lawn with gravel in the back garden. Then on the 29th April 2019 we commissioned Paul and Mark, landscape gardeners from Tasker's Gardening Services, to install oak hardwood sleepers to make three stepped graveled platforms in the bank at the roadside of our front garden. The bank was originally grassed which I had found to be more and more difficult to keep cut due to my poorly knees. Paul and Mark made a superb job of our new three terraced platforms. They also re-graveled our front drive for us. It all looked great when they finished on Tuesday 7th May 2019. We are well pleased with the end results (see above). Susie and I then dressed the platforms with plants and large flint stones and three terracotta balls just to finish it off on Thursday 9th May 2019. Today in 2020 the new feature still looks great and come through its first winter and still looks both attractive and it will save me so much pain in the future!…

August 2015

Paint Spraying our Boat and Plane!

Several years ago Susie gave me two metal wind ornaments for our garden. One is of a boat and the other is of a plane. These spin around, blown by the wind, at one end of a metal rod with a glass counter weight on the other end. They are then balanced on a central metal support that goes into the ground. Over time the paint had begun to flake off and the models were getting very rusty. So for the last job in August 2015 we decided to clean them up and give them a re-spray. To do this we used a spray can of matt black car paint. On the 29th it was a very still day with no wind. We need this because we planned to do the spraying on the lawn. First we had to shake the spray can really well before using it, put a dust sheet underneath each ornament to protect the grass and then we re-sprayed each ornament. We were very pleased with our efforts as the two models now looked like new. So after waiting four hours for the paint to dry we placed them back into our flower bed once more and sat back on the patio to admire our handy work. **Update 2020:** I am sad to say, that after five years the boat is getting very rusty and has a gapping hole in its hull and is not long for this earth and may well sink soon and be no more before the end of this year (2020). The plane on the other hand is still sound and flying above our flower bed in fine fashion. Perhaps we will invest in another can of black spray paint this year to keep it flying well into the future!…

September 2015

It's Time for some Garden Maintenance!

On the 1st September we decided that it was time to make a start at getting the garden ready for the coming winter months. The wooden fencing in the front garden needed some attention, the front drive needed weeding and the front hedge needed trimming. So armed with my drill, screws and some new pieces of wood I set about repairing and strengthening the front wooden fencing. When I had done this I weeded the drive by hand before using weed killer on the more stubborn areas of weed. This done it was time for a rest and a cup of coffee (you should always make the time for a coffee). We decided to leave the front hedge until later in September as the weather had again changed and it was now raining hard. **Update 2020:** I am very sad to say, that the above fencing was wiped out after gale force winds hit the fence and damaged it beyond repair in early 2018. We obviously replaced this wooden fencing straight away with stronger and better quality fencing which we hope will stay in place for many years to come. It has since come through two winters intact and today (08.03.2020) is still looking great!

Cut Flowers from our Garden that Susie displays Indoors

Throughout the summer months Susie has gathered flowers from our garden and displayed them inside the house. This act of bring the garden colour inside has really brightened up our house every day. She not only puts flower arrangements in our lounge and dining room but also into several small tins on our kitchen window sill (see above). So most days Susie can be seen gathering blooms from our garden borders to decorate our house with seasonal colour and smells. **Update 2020:** I am very pleased to say, that Susie has continued to collect our garden blooms every summer since the summer of 2015 . She has now started to collect cut spring flowers for display indoor from our garden again only this week (08.03.2020)…

September 2015

Witnessing the Dawn of New Life

Last year we had collar doves nesting in the tree just outside our car port, because of this we had the wonderful experience of watching their offspring take their first tentative flights into the big wide world. On the 3rd September, this year, we had the good fortune to watch this scene repeat itself once more, as the parents once again produced this year's clutch. I watched as the two young collar doves ungainly left the nest high up in the canopy of the same tree to flap their wings before making their first attempt at flying. It took them several attempts, but within a short space of time they had learnt the skills required for them to begin their independent lives. It is always a thrill to be able to witness nature at work. **Update 2020:** I am very pleased to say, that we have continued to see the wonders of nature in our garden play themselves out every year since 2015. The local birds first collect nest building materials, then they collect food for their newborns and finally the joy in watching them as they bring the young ones down into our garden to learn how to feed , fly and fend for themselves before the circle of life can begin all over again!

School's Back!

On the 4th September it was time to go back to school. Not for me you understand but for the children who attend our local school situated just over our back garden hedge. To hear the enthusiasm and the sound of happy raised voices coming from beyond our hedge once more was wonderful. I really like living where we do because of the planes that often fly over our garden from RAF Marham, which is also close by. I also like hearing the explosion of sound as the children play in the playground at breaks and lunchtimes. I think it is the fact that they are playing and running around and not using electronic gadgetry as many young and older people seem to do all the time that I like the most. They must be all the healthier for it. **Update 2020:** It is obvious to say, that over the years the joyous sounds of the school children playing nearby are still very much part of living where we do and we love it!…

September 2015

Bringing Order to an Unruly Hedge!

As the weather was fine and dry today (5th September) I decided to tame our front hedge. It had grown somewhat unruly over the summer so it was out with the hedge cutter. I always use a battery operated trimmer to avoid any risk of inadvertently cutting through a power cable so I had to fully charge up the battery first before I could make a start on the hedge. This done, I put down a ground sheet to catch the off cuts and began bringing the rampant hedge under control. Remembering not to cut it too severely as in the past I had cut our back garden hedge back to hard and killed great areas of it. After about an hour the hedge was neat and tidy and the cuttings were in our recycling bin so it was time for a rest and a cup of coffee. You should always make the time for a coffee.

Later that same day we visited Blickling Hall near Aylsham and looked around their gardens and lovely they were too!…

September 2015

Fish Pie…

Back to the Baking

Susie likes nothing better than to try out new bread, pastry, sweets or main course recipes in her kitchen. This is something I encourage her to do obviously as I get to enjoy the outcomes. We have family and friends coming to stay with us later in the month so she has spent some time looking through her countless cookery books to find exciting new menus to serve up to our guests. On the 8th September it was time for her to practice making her selected dishes which meant that for tea that day we had a new meal, fish pie, to sample and very good it was too!…

September 2015

Back to the Baking - Part 2

Featured above are just some of the delights Susie has made for us recently. **Update 2020:** I am very pleased to say, that Susie continues to bake regularly since 2015 and by 2020 she has created numerous delicious meals both starters, main courses, sweets and bread, buns, biscuits, pies and much much more. Much of the evidence for her undoubted skills is the increasing size of my waistband!…

September 2015

Back to My Studio

While Susie was busy in the kitchen I decided to go into my studio (the dining room table) and do some artwork. This was because it was a rainy day and the dogs were content to lay at my feet while I dabbled with my watercolour paints. I always start with a blank sheet of watercolour paper and paint directly onto this with watercolour paint. I do not use any pre-sketches and paint straight from my imagination. **Update 2020:** I am very pleased to say, that even today in 2020 while Susie often bakes I continue to sometimes paint and you will see some examples of my latest artwork in the last chapter of this book!…

September 2015

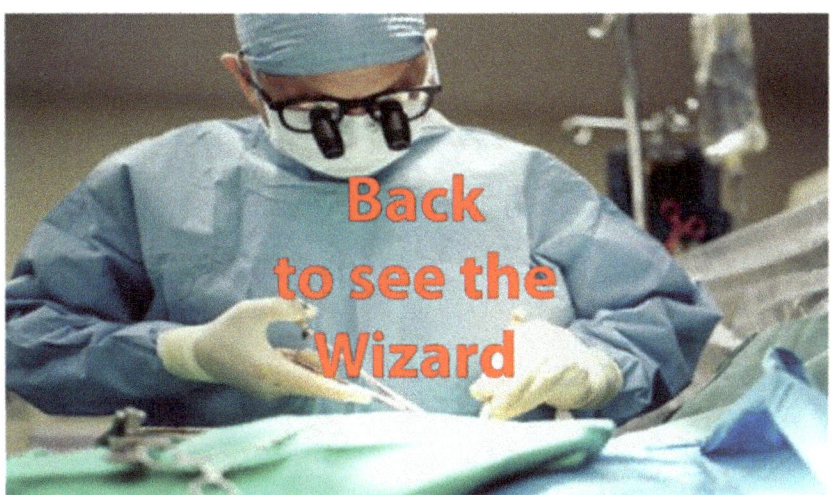

Back to See the Wizard

On Friday 11th September Susie and I went to the Queen Elizabeth Hospital in Kings Lynn to see my Orthopaedic Surgeon Mr. James Jeffery at 9 am. I had been referred back to him by my doctor because my right knee was still very painful and we were not sure what was exactly wrong with it. When we arrive we were sent to have an x-ray first before trooping in to see the wizard (Mr. James Jeffery) who after asking how my left knee replacement was doing, which he had replaced last April, he gave us the bad news that my right knee now had the same bone on bone rubbing problem as my left knee had done. He said that soon I will need to have that replaced as well. This was very sad news so after Christmas it will be back under the knife for me. **Update 2020:** I have already given you feedback on what happened next and what may have to happen in the future regarding my poorly replacement knees earlier so I think the lest said now the better!…

September 2015

Ginny and Bertie…

Poppy and Charlie…

The Dogs Big Day Out!

On Sunday 13th September we took the dogs to Sandringham (the home and grounds owned by the Queen) Country and Game fair. This is held in the grounds of the house and attracts thousands of people. We had arrange to meet Ginny and her dog Bertie there. Bertie was taking part in lurcher racing. He won one race but was disqualified from the next. We watch and were very proud of him. Our dogs dealt well with being around a lot of people for the first time and other dogs and we were very proud of them also. After spending more than three hours at the fair we made our way through the massive crowd back to the car park and returned home for some much needed peace and quiet…

September 2015

My New Book is Flying Off to the Printers

I heard from my publisher today that my 4th book to be published "Retiring to Our Garden – Year Two" has been sent to the printers for publishing. This is great news. I will receive a dozen complementary copies of the book soon so I can give them as presents to our family and friends. When I do receive these books the first copy however, will go to Mr. James Jeffery, my surgeon, as a thank you for taking the years of pain and suffering I had away from my left knee. I have dedicated this book to him and his team as a thank you. If I am lucky and get the same outcome when he operates on my right knee next year I will be well pleased. **Update 2020:** I have already given you feedback on what happened next and what may have to happen in the future regarding my poorly replacement knees earlier!…

September 2015

The Family Comes to Stay

On Thursday 24th September Susie's Mum, Sister Lou, husband Gerard and their daughter Olivia came to stay with us for a few days. Milo, their dog, also came with them. They all live in Sheffield. It was great to see them all and catch up with what they have all been up to since we last saw them. Susie made some lovely meals. We had some nice dry and warm weather so they were able to get out and about. We went to the beach at Hunstanton and drove around the lovely Norfolk countryside. **Update 2020:** I am very pleased to say, that Susie's Mum has been back every years since, usually twice a year for one week and we continue to take her out to visit interesting places in Norfolk. She came down and had Christmas 2019 with us and is due back down to stay in early June 2020. Meanwhile Susie is going up to visit her in April 2020 while the dogs and me remain at home.

Getting Ready for Christmas in September!

As we are going up to Edale in Derbyshire at the end of October, we decided to do our Christmas shopping early, so we can take our presents for the family and friends who live in and around Sheffield, with us. So on the 25th September we used the Internet to buy some gifts and then Susie went to Kings Lynn to finish off our present shopping list. By the end of the day we had managed to get all the things we wanted to give as gifts so sometime next month we will begin the massive wrapping up operation ready for them to be taken with us to Derbyshire so we can play Santa Claus in October!…

September 2015

Flying back to Africa!

Not for us you understand but for our summer guests the swallows and house martins. On the 28th September the skies above Norfolk were blue but there was no sign of the swallows and house martins that were usually swooping in the sky above us. We surmised that they have left our shore and were journeying back to Africa. They have been with us since early spring. We will miss their great flying displays, that we have watched all summer long, from our garden, but now that their young have been born and given the skills that they will need for their long flight back to Africa they have gone. The sky above us will be less interesting until they return to us once more next spring. **Update 2020:** I am very pleased to say, that the swallows and house martins continue to raise our spirits every May when they return once more to the shores of England to nest and raise their offspring. Of course they all still fly off again in September back to Africa. On a sad note there seems to be fewer and fewer of them returning to us in the last few years. I do not know why this is and can only hope that these iconic little birds recover in numbers very soon. We have really missed their wonderful flying displays that they give us as they first hunt for food to feed their offspring and then when the newborns fledge we watch them train their young in all the flying skills they will need on their long flight back to Africa. Lets hope that many more will return to our shores this year! We can not wait until May 2020 to welcome them back once more…

September 2015

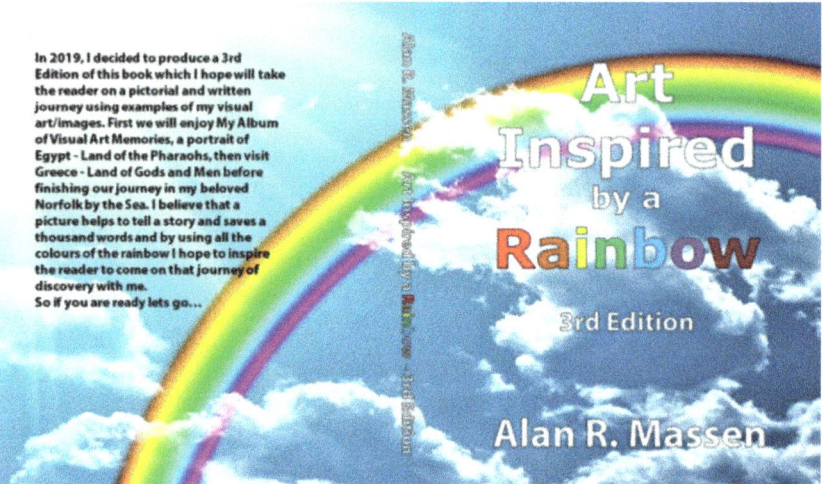

Box of Books

On the 30th September twelve copies of my latest book arrived from the publishers. With great excitement I opened the box to reveal the latest books that I have had published. The book has been published by Rainbow Publications UK. The book is called and it is about: Retiring to Our Garden – Year Two and is the continuation of the fascinating and personalised month by month pictorial tale of the dedicated creation of a beautiful Norfolk garden (ours) which is now in its second year. They say that this is a must for all plant lovers everywhere. The book looked great and so I will take a copy to Mr. James Jeffery very soon and give some of the other copies of the book as Christmas presents to my friends and family this year. **Update 2020:** I have continued giving copies of my new books as they get published to friends and family each year as gifts and the last one I gave away was at Christmas 2019 and was called Art Inspired by a Rainbow - 3rd Edition!…

October 2015

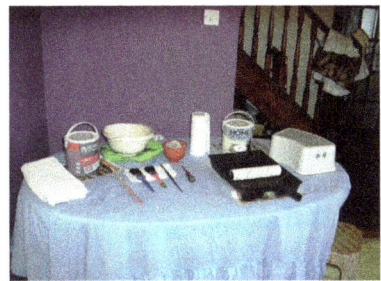 

Back to the Decorating

On the 1st October, as planned, Susie and I started to re-decorate the remaining two downstairs rooms (dining room and kitchen) that we did not do last year because of my increasing mobility problems and the severe pain that I was having with my knees last autumn/winter.

We:
- Put dust covers over dining/kitchen room floors and furniture
- Filled in all the cracks in the walls and rubbed those down when dry
- Cleaned the ceilings, walls and floors
- Masked off all of the skirting boards and power points
- Masked off ceiling fittings and front windows

When these were task done it was out with the paint, roller and brushes and on to the walls with the paint!

Back to the Decorating - Again!

We started by painting the dining room ceiling with white silk emulsion before repainting two walls of the dining room with Feather Boa (a raspberry colour) and the two remaining walls we did with a Classic Cream matt emulsion. The dining room painting took us two days to complete and then we moved into the kitchen and after masking, cleaning and covering up furniture. We repainted the walls in the kitchen with the left over paint we had from the dining room that was called Classic Cream matt emulsion. Although it had taken us four full days to complete the re-decoration of these two rooms it has been well worth it…

October 2015

The New Curtains and a Rug

As well as re-decorating the walls and ceiling we wanted to replace the dining room curtains and floor rug. After spending some time on the Internet we selected a new pair of curtains and a large patterned rug. The curtains came very quickly, so on the 5th October Susie put the new curtains, in the dining room and they looked lovely. She had also ordered a new large rug for under our dining room table but unfortunately this had not yet arrived. We later learnt that it was temporarily out of stock but would be with us by early November so we will have to wait awhile longer to completely finish how we want the dining room to look after its recent re-decoration…

October 2015

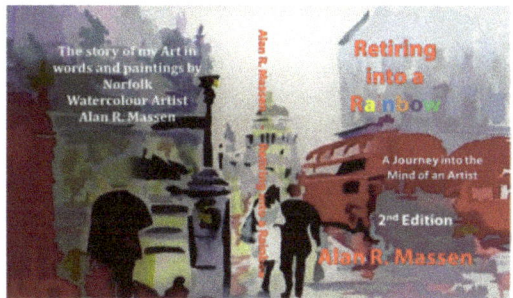
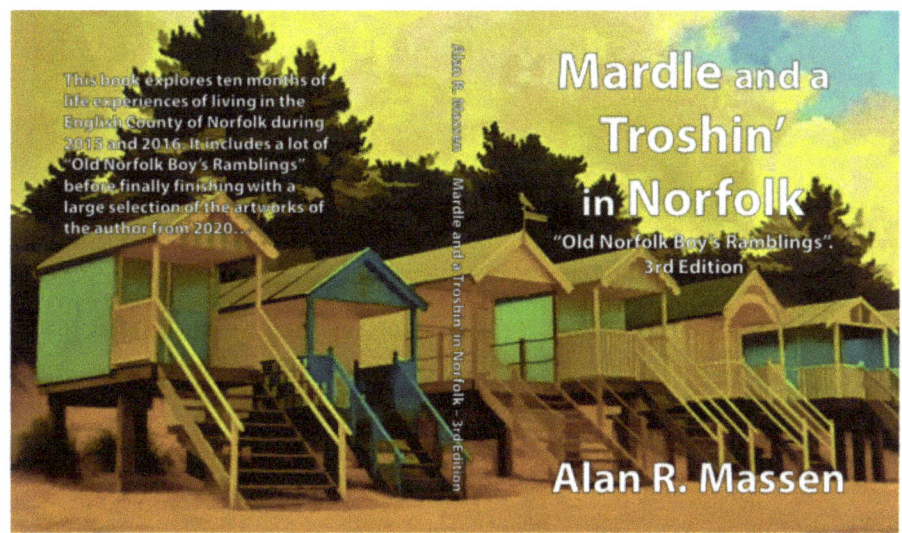

Doubling Up to a Treble

My publisher Rainbow Publications UK and I have decided to re-issue my first two books as second editions: Retiring to Our Garden Year One and Retiring into a Rainbow. This has meant that I have spent the last two days revising the content and inserting some new artwork into each book. When I had finished this I re-submitted my two 2nd editions for approval. This took a further couple of days but the process was successful and so the new editions were sent off to the printers for publication. I will receive an electronic proof copy of each of the books to review and approve before they go on general sale in America, Canada, Australia, Europe, rest of the World and of course in the UK! **Update 2020:** I am still writing most days and this year alone I have already completed writing and having published three books to-date! I have today 2nd March 2020 just started my updating of this 3rd Edition book called Mardle and a Troshin in Norfolk!…

October 2015

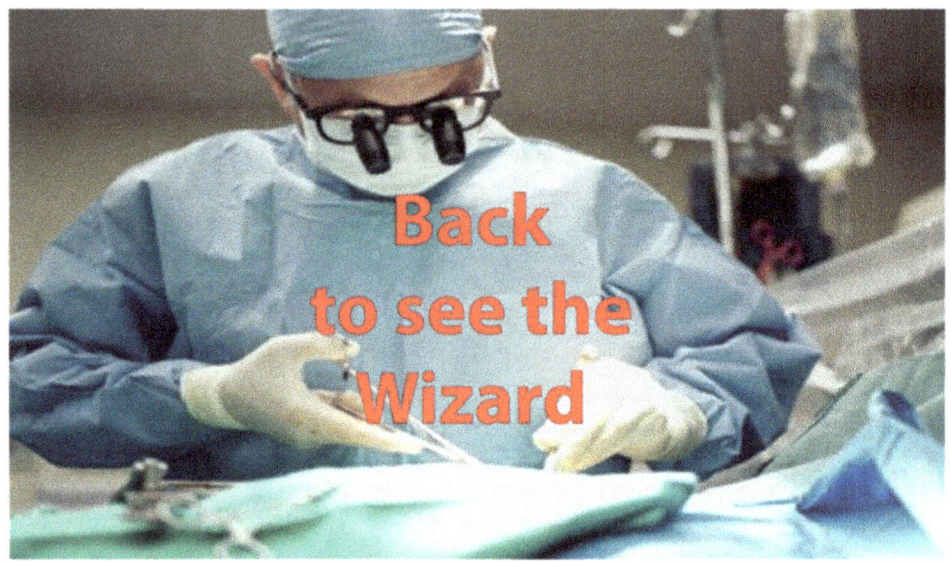

I'm Off to See the Wizard Once More Bearing Gifts

I did not have an appointment, but on Friday 9th October, I took a signed copy of my first book and my latest book to the Queen Elizabeth Hospital to give to Mr. James Jeffery. I had already given him a signed copy of my second book "Retiring into a Rainbow" when I was in hospital recovering from my knee surgery in early April. He was very please to receive that gift and after all he has done such a great job of my operation I decided to give him two more of my books as a thank you gift. He was well pleased and he later sent me a lovely thank you letter. **Update 2020:** Enough said already but I hope that I will not be seeing him anytime soon!...

October 2015

Putting our Garden to Bed

After I returned from the hospital to deliver my books to Mr. James Jeffery, Susie and I decided to make a start at putting the garden to bed for the coming winter. As a starting point we tidied up the greenhouse and patio pots before cutting back some of the large shrubs in our back garden. Once we had done this and as the weather was sunny and warm we went and sat up on the decking with the dogs and enjoyed some snacks and a cold drink. **Update 2020:** We have continued to put our garden to bed every year since. Obviously every year in spring we wake our garden up again by refreshing/replacing the soil and planting new plants in our pots, planting new tomato plants in the greenhouse and generally tidying up the garden after it has laid dormant during the winter!…

October 2015

Playtime!

On the 10th October Susie spent the afternoon playing with the dogs Poppy and Charlie on our back garden lawn. This is something she does most days and the dogs really love it. I was sitting on the decking watching them playing so well and decided to take a photograph of the fun. My camera, was to-hand, and I took the above pictures. The noises they all made and the happy tail wags all made it obvious that they were enjoying themselves. Susie as well minus the tail wagging!

Bertie and Ginny Comes to Stay

On Sunday 12th October Ginny and Bertie had gone to a lurcher show at Peterborough and came and stayed the night with us after it finished. Our dogs love it when Bertie comes to stay and especially Charlie who views Bertie as his personal tall play mate. After staying the night Ginny left the next morning and we settled down to await the arrival of our very good friends Andrew and Lynn with their dog Franky…

October 2015

My paintings of Baz and Franky…

Andy, Lynn and Franky are Coming

On Sunday 13th at 3 pm, Andrew and Lynn with their dog Franky arrived. They will be staying with us overnight before returning to their home just outside Sheffield. After we had one of Susie famously delicious meals and several drinks we all settled down to watch a film in the evening. The next morning everyone, except me (poorly knees), took the dogs to the local dog walking woods before having breakfast. After a good chat they left on their long journey home. It was great to see them all and we arranged to go to their house when we go up to Edale in late October. **Update 2020:** I am very pleased to say, that we have visited Andy and Lynn at theirs and they have return to visit us several times since 2015. The only difference recently is that they have added to their family. They still go to The Troulos Bay Hotel on Skiathos every year and in 2017 they returned back home with a Friend! They now have a Greek dog called Baz and just like Franky I painted a picture of Baz which now it is proudly displayed on their kitchen/dining room wall (see above). Sadly Frank died in February 2020. He will be greatly missed…

October 2015

My Book: Retiring to Our Garden Year One - 2nd Edition is published

On the 14th October I received my proof copy of my 2nd edition book "Retiring to Our Garden – Year One". I liked the new cover that I had used for this re-issue and I thought that it was better than the first edition that featured a picture of me on the front cover (see below):

The draft copy of my new book looked great and after reviewing it I confirmed that I was happy with it to my publisher who will now release it for general sale…

October 2015

My Book: Retiring into a Rainbow - 2nd Edition is published

On the 15th October I received my proof copy of my 2nd edition book "Retiring into a Rainbow". It looked great and after reviewing it I confirmed that I was happy with it to my publisher who will now release it for general sale. **Update 2020:** As the years have passed by and I have written more books we have continued to use this process for all of my subsequent books. It has worked very well so I will continue to write my books, the publisher will then review the draft and produce a proof copy that I will review and if I am happy he will then release the final version of the book for general sale on Amazon and other good book retailers!…

October 2015

Getting Taped Up - All Wrapped Up

As we approach our late October holiday to Edale in Derbyshire, Susie and I decided to wrap up all the Christmas presents that we want to take with us to give to family and friends. This took us all afternoon but we managed to complete the wrapping of all of the gifts by the end of the day. Let's hope that after all this we remember to take them with us when we go!

Bed Time - Putting the Garden Ornaments Away

On the 19th October I decide that I would put all the vulnerable garden ornaments into our shed so they will be protected from the winter cold and frost. It took me several hours to complete this task and when I finished I asked Susie to check that I had found and put away everything. She of course found that I had indeed missed several ornaments, so she help me put the last few away. When we return from our holiday to Edale in Derbyshire we will only have one last pre-winter job to do in the garden. This is to put the last few patio potted plants that we want to protect from the ravages of winter into the greenhouse. Then we will have finished putting our garden to bed for this year. **Update 2020:** Like every other year since 2015 we will retrieved our plants from the greenhouse and our ornaments from the shed in early May 2020 and place them in the garden for another year in the summer sun shine (we hope)!…

October 2015

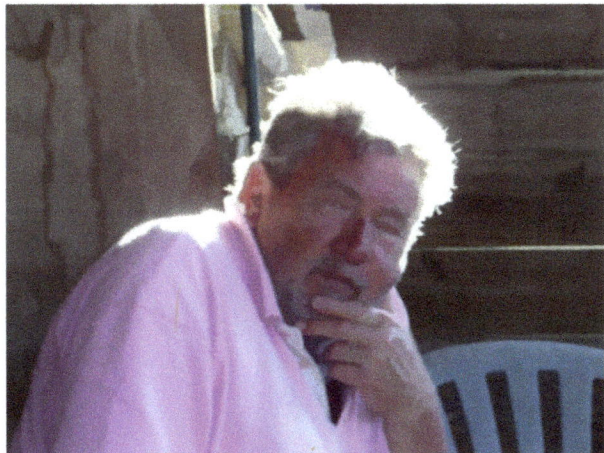

Alan at rest in 2015 and 2020…

Last Cut of the Year?

On Tuesday 20th October I have mowed the lawn for the last time this year! Susie has had to take over many of the gardening tasks this year including keeping the lawn cut. This is because of my lack of mobility due to the problems that I have had with my knees. Even though my right knee is still very painful and I find it difficult to walk very far I thought that as Susie was at work today and the weather was going to be heavy rain tomorrow I would try and cut the grass to save her a job. This could also be the last chance we get to keep the grass under control before we go away on holiday on Friday to Derbyshire. So I made a start after all how hard could it be? I soon found out as my knee soon told me to stop, so after just 30 minutes I had cut just a third of the lawn. I had a sit on the decking with the now somewhat amused dogs for 20 minutes and then I tried again. I managed to complete the cutting of the lawn after two further rest periods but then had to sit on the decking for another two hour before I could bear to move once more. Susie got home from work and was well pleased with my efforts but boy didn't I suffer that night with not much sleep and a lot of pain…

October 2015

Off to Edale in Derbyshire

On Friday 23rd October Susie and I set off for our holiday cottage in Barber Booth near Edale in Derbyshire. The car was loaded to the gunnels with two dogs and their beds and other essential items (FOOD) such as bedding, leads, coats and oh yes dog food. The car also had to coup with our case of cloths, our box of food, Christmas presents and many other essential items. By the time Susie and I got into the car it was full to overflowing. So with everything packed we set off on our first holiday with Poppy and Charlie. This was set to be a great adventure for us ALL. Edale is a valley in North Derbyshire about 15 miles west of Sheffield in the heart of the Peak National Park. Much of the surrounding land is preserved for the nation by the National Trust. Visitors from all over the nation and the wider world visit the valley, every year, which is in the centre of some of the finest walking country in England…

October 2015

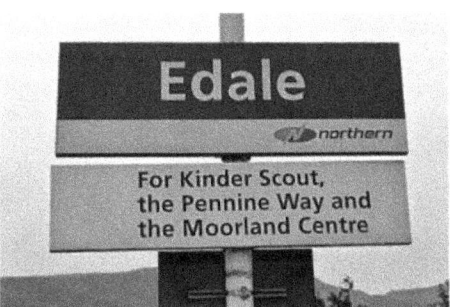

Station Sign and the Entrance to the Pennine Way in the village of Edale

The History of Edale and the Surrounding Area

Close to Edale an Iron Age hill fort was built on Mam Tor, near Castleton, and later the Romans built a fort at the entrance of the dale near Hope. In medieval times packhorses were used to carry heavy loads over the hills. A "Jagger" was the name for the man in charge of a packhorse train. From the 1700's water became the source of energy that drove the industrial revolution. Richard Arkwright, a famous name in these parts, started to build cotton mills in the Derbyshire dales. Edale was an isolated farming community at this time but in 1792 a cotton mill was built in the dale. It closed in 1934. In 1894 the railway was built between Manchester and Sheffield with the line running through Edale. The railway help make the Peak District accessible for city dwellers and the Pennine Way begins beside the Nags Head public house in the village of Edale…

October 2015

Susie and the Dogs out and about in Edale

A Rainy Day in Edale

The landscape around the village of Edale consists of high hills such as Nether Tor, Jaggers Clough and Jacobs Ladder surround the valley, the river Noe runs through it. A real feature of the area is the dry stone walls that are used to segregate the fields and keep the animals from roaming too far. A large number of ramblers and walkers start their Pennine walk adventure from here. It also rains a lot!…

October 2015

The Boothies (Booths) of Edale

Boothies or Booths were the original temporary shelters for boothmen, who were in charge of livestock kept on the surrounding hills. Edale has five Booths. Nether and Upper Booths with Ollerbrook Booth, Grindsbrook Booth and Barber Booth were the cottage we stayed in was called "The Old Dairy" is located (see above)…

October 2015

The Flora and Fauna of the Edale Area

The flora and fauna of the Edale area: the Rowan tree, mosses and Ling Heather. These plants are just about all that can be sustained on the hills above Edale. In the hills above Edale you may spot the following fauna: rabbits, grouse and black and white dippers. If you are really lucky you may see the wild mountain hare but sightings are now very rear. The fields below the hills are full of cows and hardy sheep such as Swaledale, Blue Faced Leicester's or the Derbyshire Gritstone breed…

October 2015

Our Holiday to the Derbyshire High Dales

Friday 23rd October: We arrived at our cottage in Barber Booth at 4 pm after driving for about four hours all the way from Norfolk. The dogs were very well behaved and we settled into this, what turned out to be, a well-equipped cottage for the night wondering what delights we had awaiting us in the morning…

October 2015

Our Holiday to the Derbyshire High Dales

Day One - Saturday 24th October: It was raining hard so Susie went shopping for fresh food into Castleton before we explored some of the local walks with our dogs. In the afternoon, as the rain had stopped, we went into Edale village and walked a short distance on the Pennine Way before returning to the village for our lunch which we had in the Nags Head. The dogs behaved themselves very well and the pub grub was delicious…

October 2015

Our Holiday to the Derbyshire High Dales

Day Two - Sunday 25th October: We decided to spend the day at our friends Andrew and Lynn, who live in Mosborough, just outside of Sheffield, with their dog Franky. It was only just about an hour away from Barber Booth. Lynn cooked us a great meal and their house was lovely. The dogs went out with Franky for a long walk off their leads which they loved. Later we sat on their patio and enjoyed a drink and a good chat before returning to our cottage, once more, in the late afternoon. **Update 2020:** As I have already mentioned in 2017, 2018 and 2019 they went to stay at the fabulous Troulos Bay Hotel on the Greek Island of Skiathos. In 2017 They returned back home with a Friend! A Greek Beagle dog called Baz. Just as I had done with Franky I painted a picture of Baz, which now, I am proud to say is displayed on their kitchen/dining room wall. As already mentioned Franky died in February 2020 however, Andy and Lynn plan to return once more to Skiathos in June 2020. We hope that they have another great holiday at Troulos Bay Hotel on this paradise Greek island…

October 2015

Bakewell…

Our Holiday to the Derbyshire High Dales

Day Three - Monday 26th October: Today we decided to visit the Derbyshire market town of Bakewell as it was market day there and it should be an interesting day out. The weather was very sunny and warm so it was very pleasant driving through the Dales. We had to wait some time to get into the car park as the place was packed. We had a great lunch at the Castle Inn before buying ourselves a famous Bakewell Pudding to take home. As we were all tired we left the town and had a pleasant drive through the Derbyshire countryside before returning back to Barber Booth tired but please at our day out in Bakewell…

October 2015

Our Holiday to the Derbyshire High Dales

Day Four - Tuesday 27th October: After yesterday's visit to Bakewell, where I managed to twist my right knee badly, I was in severe pain all night so our only excursion out today was to go and meet Susie's Mum and sister in law Kate for lunch. It was really great to see them both and we had a nice catch up chat. We meet at the Millstone Country Inn (top picture) which is just outside Hathersage (bottom picture). The food we had was very good and the dogs once more were great…

October 2015

Our Holiday to the Derbyshire High Dales

Day Five - Wednesday 28th October: As my knee is still very painful we have decided to travel home a day early so we will not be able to see our daughter Mandy and her husband Adrian as we had hoped to do. Today our only expedition out was to go to the Bulls Head pub in Monyash to have lunch with Susie sister Lou, husband Gerard and their daughter Olivia. It was really great to see them all once again and after a very good pub meal it was time to bid them a fond farewell and head back to our cottage for the last night of our stay!…

October 2015

Our House…

Poppy and Charlie…

Homeward Bound

Day Six - Thursday 29th October: Today we packed our things and headed home to Norfolk. During our stay Susie has walked the dogs at least three or four times a day usually for three or four miles at a time. The dogs have enjoyed this but on the down side they have had to stay on their leads all the time because of all the sheep and other animals roaming the hills. The Old Dairy Cottage has been an ideal base and we have enjoyed our stay there. The scenery has been spectacular and the warmth of the people has made our stay here very enjoyable indeed. We arrived home safely and it was time to reflect on our week in the Derbyshire high dales. We were very proud of how well our dogs had dealt with this new experience. They had been great on their leads, in the car and been very patient whilst we had our pub meals. All in all, we had a lovely time, and look forward to returning one day. This will largely depend on having my knee surgery on my now very painful right knee as soon as possible. We hope to return to Derbyshire in the not to distant future. **Update 2020:** As I have already mentioned I had my partial right knee replacement operation in 2016 but I am sad to say we have not returned to Derbyshire since we went in 2015. Maybe some day!…

November 2015

Sitting in the Sun all Day!

Sunday 1st November and the sun was out and the sky was blue so after Susie and I had put several of the pots from the patio into the greenhouse to over winter we retired to our decking to sunbathe for the rest of the day with the dogs. It was a real treat sitting in the sun all day in November. That's right November!

Back to my Writing!

In early November I started writing notes about our recent holiday in Derbyshire ready for there inclusion into this book. As I did so I thought that I would include a brief outline of one of the walks you could undertake, if unlike me, you are fit and have a strong sense of adventure. The Pennine Way has a reputation for dropping you in at the deep end. Literally, if the weather is particularly bad. Susie and I did start this walk when we were in Edale last month but I found the going too tough for my poorly knee and we soon abandoned it and went back to the Nags Head pub for an early lunch and a few pints of beer. If we had continued our walk we would have been on the walk described on the next few pages…

November 2015

Walking the Pennine Way starting at Edale

The walk: Walking from Edale to Glossop or should I say "taking a long hike" you will find the first section, like the three that follow, takes you over some of the toughest terrain in Britain (peat moorland).

If you are ready let's get started: Kinder Scout, the upland plateau crossed by this first section of the Pennine Way, is a large area of blanket bog. The plateau is virtually flat, which means that rainwater has nowhere to run; the soil, naked peat, soaks up this water like a giant sponge and retains it for weeks. Much of Kinder is permanently saturated (much like us whenever we ventured out into the hills around Edale). It's quite usual for walkers on this plateau to find themselves sinking into black mud up to their knees, or even worse (sounds like fun to me). There have been occasions on which unwary or inexperienced walkers have sunk up to their waists, or even their chests, and become trapped. Although, they say, nobody has actually drowned in this fashion it's entirely possible to succumb to exposure as a consequence. Fatalities have occurred be warned! Taking a mobile phone fully charged may prove a life saver!…

November 2015

Walking the Pennine Way starting at Edale

It's easy, however, to paint too black a picture of Kinder Scout. Crossing it safely is simply a matter of common sense. Remember fools rush in so plan before you go! If in doubt, catch the train at Edale station and go under the high peaks by train instead! If you're used to the terrain you'll know exactly what to expect. If you've never encountered peat moorland before, then avoid crossing it in bad weather. If you must attempt the crossing during or after rain, don't go alone or better still, stick to the "bad weather route" along the edge of the plateau. In fine, settled weather the moorland crossing is an enjoyable adventure many would say. So if the suns out get your boots on! The standard Pennine Way guidebooks would have you crossing both Kinder Scout and Bleaklow, the next moorland area to the north, on the same day. If you are an experienced and fit hiker, if you're not pushed for time and have to get the miles in, then by all means walk them both. Let us assumes otherwise, that, for instance, you've spent half the morning just travelling to Edale, that you've spent the greater part of the year sitting at a desk or a bench or the wheel of a car and are not particularly fit like me, and that you're not used to the rigours of moorland walking which I am not. Then turn to the next page for some sound advice…

November 2015

Walking the Pennine Way starting at Edale

In any of these circumstances it's better to fix Snake Pass as the end of the day's walk and Glossop as your eventual destination. I think that eight and a half miles is plenty on your first day. The walk from Edale to Snake Pass divides down more or less into three subsections, of which the crossing of Kinder is the central part. From the start at Edale you first have to ascend to the plateau. There were originally two routes; the "official" route by way of Grindsbrook Clough, and the "alternative" bad-weather route via Upper Booth. The latter alternative is now the "official" route, although purists will wish to stick to Grindsbrook. Grindsbrook has fine ravine scenery. Eagle-eyed map readers will spot a third alternative, a local footpath ascending the spur of land between the two aforementioned valley routes. This path, up Grindslow Knoll, might well find favour if you wish to avoid the crowds or simply wish to be different. A tip: take a map with you and a compass. Trying to read your map and compass will be such fun and they may even save your life. I promise!…

November 2015

Walking the Pennine Way starting at Edale

Having reached the plateau proper, you now have the choice of crossing it (if you ascended via Grindsbrook Clough or Grindslow Knoll), or taking the "bad weather" path around the edge (mandatory if you ascended via Upper Booth, optional otherwise). Kinder is a great place to be on a fine, dry day. Many people expect moors to be featureless. Kinder is anything but. It's a riot of vegetation, for one thing. There is mat grass and heather, ling, gorse, bilberry and a gamut of other wild shrubs, not to mention the host of alpines and bog flowers that thrive here. Topologically, too, it's anything but dull. Although the plateau is flat overall, locally it's a maze of knolls, hillocks, hummocks and sinewy watercourses known as peat groughs. These can be a real sod to cross. Typically, a crossing involves a muddy descent of anything between six and twenty feet to reach the floor, followed by an even steeper, wetter and muddier climb out. That sounds like fun but it is not my idea of fun but as they say it takes all sorts! Sounds like a real mud bath to me! **Update 2020:** I have included, on this page, a watercolour painting that I did in 2018 of a group of walkers setting off to walk the Pennine Way from Edale…

November 2015

Walking the Pennine Way starting at Edale

On this walk don't expect to stay clean except under drought conditions. When we were there in October it rained most (every) days. If crossing them it is difficult, walking along them can be a joy. The bigger and deeper ones tend to have cut right through the peat to reach firm, silty beds that make first class paths. This sounds like real fun! The direct and bad-weather routes converge at Kinder Downfall, four miles out of Edale. Susie and the dogs walked this distance on most days that we were in the high peaks. I did not! I think that if, by a miracle, I had reach this point I would have headed straight back to the warmth of the pub and a good meal…

November 2015

Alan safely back in the pub…

Walking the Pennine Way starting at Edale

If, unlike me, you are still marching along the path that follows the edge of the moor for another mile before descending steeply to the Ashop Clough col. From the col the path enters the third and final sub-stage of the walk, along the lonely and drab moraine ridge of Mill Hill and Featherbed Moss. There is little to be said about this two and a half mile stretch. It is featureless and it is sloppy. So maybe my idea of giving this a miss is a wise one! The main Snake Pass (A57) road is visible throughout. Once you reach the tarmac turn left and walk down to Glossop. Muddy but with the warm glow of your achievement fresh in your mind. I admire you the adventurer for making this hike or to you who may do in the future I say good luck you mad fools. May the force be with you!…

November 2015

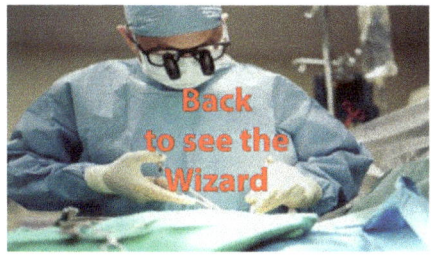 

Referral Back to See the Wizard

There has been no improvement in my right knee pain since we returned from our holiday so on Monday 2nd November I spoke to my GP doctor Kant and asked him to refer me back to see Mr. James Jeffery my Orthopaedic Surgeon as soon as possible. My doctor agreed and said that he would organise a referral back to see my surgeon in the near future. I hope that this will mean that I will have a knee replacement operation sometime in early 2016. This will mean that both of my knees will be bionic (made of metal)! So now it is just a matter of me waiting for the N.H.S to contact me with an appointment date and time so I can go to the Queen Elizabeth hospital, Kings Lynn, to get this sorted out once and for all. In the afternoon the rug that we had ordered for the dining room floor arrived and looked great when we laid it down. This was the final touch to this room which we finished re-decorating a few weeks ago. **Update 2020:** As you know by now I am now the bionic man official. What's that you might say "We can rebuild him but why bother". Harsh but true!

Walking in Shouldham Warren

On the 8th November Ginny, Bertie, Susie, Poppy, Charlie and me went for a long walk in the Warren which is near our village in Norfolk…

November 2015

Alan in Shades…

Sixty-Six - Not Out

No I have not taken up playing cricket but this month I celebrated the sixty-sixth year of my life. So I am another year older. For my birthday, I received from Susie's Mum Ann, a dog ornament for our garden, which we named Poppy as it looked a lot like our dog Poppy. Andy and Lynn gave me six bottles of beer and a box of sweets. Ginny gave me a Bonsai tree, whilst Susie gave me a shooting stick, a new coffee mug, a grow your own chrysanthemum kit and the latest Jack Reacher book by Lee Child called "Make Me". This book completes my collection of all the books he has published to date. I cannot wait to get started on Reacher's latest adventure. **Update 2020:** This year I have reached the ripe old age of seventy (70th birthday on the 03.11.2019). As it is only April 2020 at the moment, I do not know what present(s) I may be lucky enough to get this year but I already have all a man can reasonably hope for: A beautiful and loving wife Susie, great friends, reasonably good health except for poorly knees and my team Norwich City FC have just been promoted back to the Premier League (well until later this year perhaps). It just can not get any better than this can it!…

November 2015

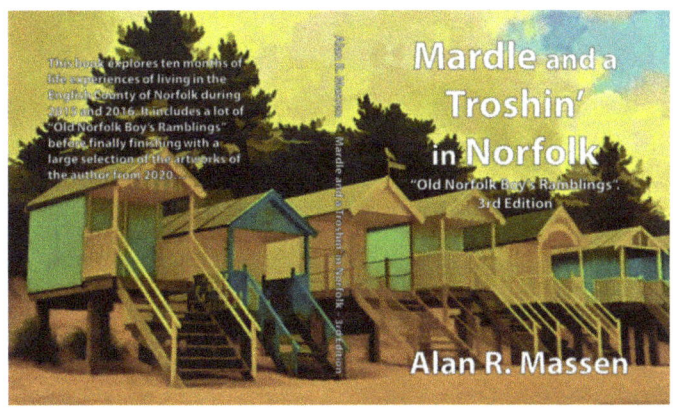

Another One Bites the Dust

To celebrate my recent birthday I spent the 6th and 7th November finishing the draft of my latest book that is called "Skiathos a Greek Island Paradise - 2nd Edition". This done I submitted it to my publisher "Rainbow Publications UK". Once it has been edited and I have approved the proof it will be sent onto the printers for printing. I really enjoyed writing about Skiathos, our holiday paradise and cannot wait to see what our Greek friends make of it! **Update 2020:** This year I have up-dated this book "Mardle and a Troshin' in Norfolk - 3rd Edition" and will re-publish it in May 2020. I will also reach my seventy first birthday in November 2020…

November 2015

A New Project!

Having completed my latest book on Skiathos I spent some time thinking about what to write about next. Then as often happens to me I just knew what I was going to do next! So today (9th November) I started to plan my next book which I am going to call "Norfolk the County of my Birth". It will feature the history and a journey around the county of my birth in words and pictures. I also plan to include my personal reminisces and memories of me growing up and living in my beautiful home county. I am really excited about my new project so must stop typing and get on with the writing! **Update 2020:** Once again this year I have up-dated one of my 2015 books and re-published it as a 2nd Edition (see above). I will probably revise all my earlier titles to keep them up to date this year!...

November 2015

Alan thinking…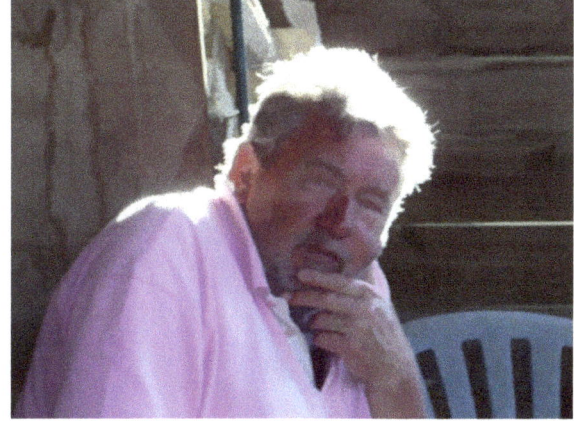

Parting is Such Sweet Sorrow!

It is always sad to say goodbye to someone of something you love. On the 11th November I had to do just that. Today I took my beloved car to be sold. It was hard to part with my faithful car after eight years of great service and I shall miss it greatly. As my right knee continues to get more and more painful, and I am finding it harder and harder to drive the car, due to the pain, and as I will be going under the knife once more early next year it was time for it to go. I would have found it more and more difficult in the future to keep my car roadworthy as I would not be able to drive it very much after my surgery for several months so it was time for us to part. So it's goodbye from the car and it's goodbye from me! Just for now but turn a page and I am back!…

December 2015

The Last Cut - Well Maybe!

On the 1st December Susie helped by Charlie and Poppy mowed our lawn for the last time this year we hope. **Update 2020:** Although we have reduced the amount of lawn in our back garden and eliminated the grass bank at the front of our house this ritual of cutting the grass is very much still part of our lives even today!…

December 2015

The Home Brew!

No not a cup or pot of tea but in early December 2015 Susie and I decided that we would start making our own home made wine, once more, after many years. We had all the equipment to do this in our loft. We just had to buy ourselves a deep rich red (6 bottle kit) and a Rosé wine (30 bottle kit). We started our brews off on the 2nd December. It should be ready in about seven to ten days time. So it will be ready just in time for the Christmas celebrations! **Update 2020:** Although we did continued to make our own reasonably tasting wine for a couple of years we decided in 2018 that it took up to much space in our already crowded kitchen so we reverted back to buying it ready made. So it was back to the loft for the kit and off to the shops for us!…

December 2015

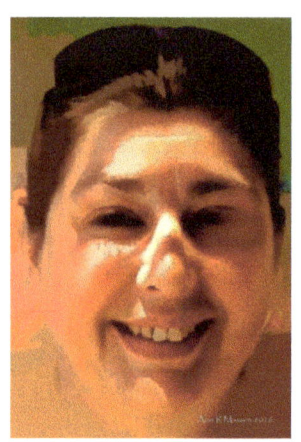

I am very proud to announce that WE HAVE STOPPED!

Giving it Up for a Better Life

On Wednesday 25th November I stopped smoking and on Friday 27th November Susie also stopped smoking. We have been talking about stopping for some time. I mainly stopped because I will be having surgery again early in the New Year and not smoking will help me recover quicker (I also stopped before my last operation in April but started again after six weeks). Susie has stopped mainly to help save money so she can keep working part time next year. We were originally going to quit at the end of the year but decided why wait to save money and also gain health wise. I waited a week before I wrote this up **just in case** we failed but I am pleased to report that both Susie and I have not had a single cigarette and are now **SMOKE FREE! Update 2020:** We are both proud to say that we have Kicked the Habit and We Have NOT Smoked Since November 2015 which is more than four years now!…

December 2015

All wrapped Up!

On Monday 8th December I spent the day wrapping up Susie's Christmas presents. I cannot tell you what I will be giving her just in case she reads my notes before Xmas morning. Once I had finished wrapping all her gifts up I managed to put them away just minutes before Susie arrived back home from work. **Update 2020:** I like to buy my presents for Susie early and wrap them up so she cannot easily see what I have bought for her. I have continued to do this every year we have been married however, this year I have really surpassed myself because here we on the 10th April 2020 and I have already purchased her birthday, anniversary, Christmas and valentine presents for the year ahead. I have also wrapped them up and put them in a place of safety to await these special days. I am very good don't you think and it takes being prepared to a whole new level!…

December 2015

Christmas Lunch with my Sisters

On Wednesday 16th December Susie and I drove to the Red Lion PH in Eaton just outside Norwich to meet my sisters Phyllis and Doreen and their husbands Tony and Dennis for our annual Christmas lunch together. This is the second year we have been to this pub and we enjoyed our meal there again this year. It was really nice to see them all and exchange Christmas gifts at this special time. **Update 2020:** Every year since we have continued this tradition until two years and now we exchange gifts by post. X-rays of both my knees in November 2018 identified that my left knee was likely to collapse. My GP then made an urgent appointment for me to see my surgeon Mr. Jeffery. I cancelled our Xmas lunch due to this risk. I went to see my surgeon on the 14th December 2018 and and again on the 12th December 2019 what he told me - I will tell you on the next page!…

December 2015

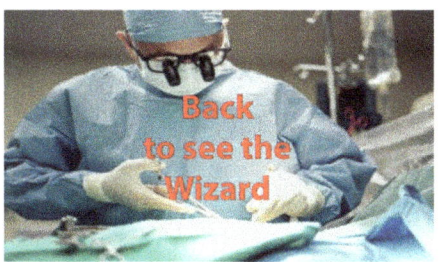 

I'm Off to see the wizard (ONCE AGAIN)!

On Friday 18th December Susie and I went to see my surgeon Mr. James Jeffery at the Queen Elizabeth Hospital in Kings Lynn at 9.40 am. On this same day our very good friend Lynn also went into hospital in Sheffield for an operation. So as we travelled to my appointment our thoughts were with Lynn and her husband Andy. After an x-ray, physical examination and discussion it was decided that I would have to wait until I had lost some weight before having my right knee replaced, as the surgeon was not happy to proceed until I had got my weight below 100 kg (currently 118 kg). We went home somewhat despondently as I was in a lot of pain and getting the weight down was going to be a big challenge but hey hoe we had stop smoking so this should be a doodle! We soon cheered up however, when we spoke to Andy and Lynn in the evening and found out that her operation had gone very well. So that was some very good news. Susie and I decided, that evening, that we would start a diet in the New Year, so I could reduce my weight, as soon as possible, thus allowing me to have my knee replacement operation done as soon as possible. **Update 2020:** As you know by now I lost the 18 kg in weight and had my right partial knee replacement done in April 2016 but life has a strangle way of repeating itself sometimes. The appointment on the 18th December 2018 was mirrored with another one I had with him on the 14th December 2019 to get his opinion. This was as a direct result of the report on the x-rays I had which said that my left knee was likely to collapse. Mr Jeffery examined both my knees and had a really good look at the x-rays. He was happy with their current condition but added that he felt that there could be some thinning of the bone which could be a problem in the future. This could lead to a potential collapse of the replacement knee joint sometime in the future that would then require additional surgery. He also said that he would see me again every year to formally review the ongoing condition of the replacement knee joints. I now feel somewhat reassured that my knees are not likely to collapse on me any time soon! Today they are increasingly painful and recently I had to go back onto the strongest pain killing medication while I await further surgery. The main problem is that my replacement knees wake me up about every two to three hours every night. I then have to take more painkilling tablets to get back to sleep only to be awoken once more in agony. The sleep loss is proving to be wearisome and I am unhappy at having to take so many drugs!…

December 2015

A Happy Christmas and New Year from US to YOU

Goodbye from the year 2015 and welcome in the year 2016. I have finished this month's rambling by including above the six seasonal offerings for your amusement and I will see you all again next **YEAR in January 2016**…

January 2016
Welcome Back and a Happy New Year

Santa on his bike!

Susie, and I, had a lovely Christmas, and received loads of nice presents, but now that Christmas is over, we must all look forward to, and hope for, a better and healthier New Year ahead. On the 1st January Susie, the dogs and I went for our first walk of the year, in the woods at Shouldham Warren. Today we shared the woods with not just other dog walkers, horses and recreation cyclist but a cycling club having their post- Christmas cycle races. It was very amusing to see that many of them had dressed up for the event (see above) with some in Santa outfits. We had a lovely long walk and then returned home to enjoy the first day of our diet. We have decided to fast on two days a week and just reduce our normal meals on the other five days. It will be interesting to see how this works out. I am pleased to say both Susie and I have managed to not smoke at all since we stopped in late November so we are well pleased. I can also report that the wine that we brewed came out really well and is/was very nice. We made more than 36 bottles so we have not finished it yet but we will start some more off later in the month. Just in case! We still have not had any snow as yet this winter although we have had a lot of rain but the weather has been unusually warm for this time of year!…

January 2016

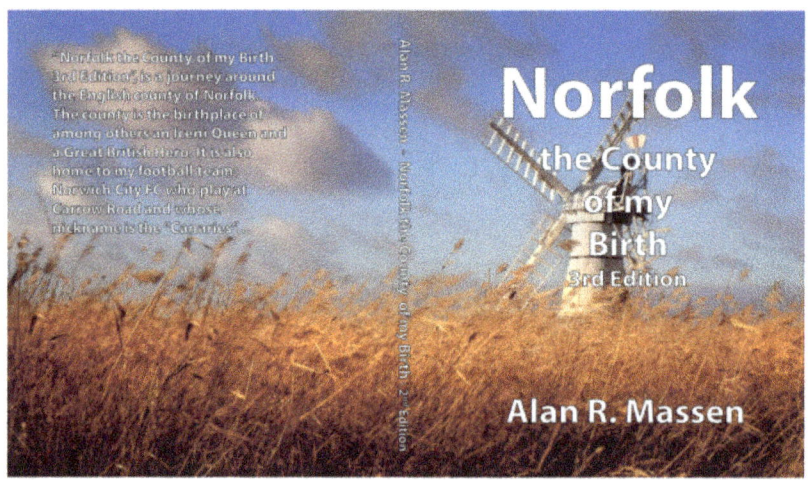

Back to my Writing!

Early this month I completed the drafts, editing and sent to my publisher my latest two books. The books are entitled "Skiathos a Greek Island Paradise" and "Norfolk the County of my Birth". These are the 7th and 8th books that I will have had published to-date. The first book is about the Greek island that we have gone to for many years for our summer holidays. The second journeys around Norfolk and includes many of my memories of growing up in this wonderful English County. **Update 2020:** This year I plan to update and re-publish all of my twenty paperback books as 3rd editions during March, April, May and June 2020. To-date (3rd May) I have managed to complete the re-publication of eight of my 3rd Editions books!…

January 2016

Brewing, Dieting without Shortness of Breathe!

We have been steadily working our way through the first batch of our home brew wine that we made, and before we finish this off, we thought that we ought to get the next batch on the way, so by the time we need it the new batch will be ready. So following the success of our first batch of home brewed wine, we decided, on the 15th January that we would started another wine home brew kit off today. We decided to use the same kit as before that makes 30 bottles of rosé wine as it made such a fine tasting wine. We also started our diet on the 1st of January. As planned, and on the first day I weighed 118 kg but by the 15th January this was down to 115 kg and by the 31st January it stood at 110 kg. This is great and hopefully, I will be down below 100 kg in the next few months, thus enabling me to have my right knee replacement operation, as planned. Susie has also been on the diet and she has also lost 6 kg to date. Another one of Susie and my big success stories this month has been that we have succeeded in not having any cigarettes at all since mid-November last year. We are both rightly proud of our achievement and both feel that we are over the craving and we will continue to be smoke free in the future. So a big pat on the back for each of us and no more puffs of smoke for us.

A Greater Spotted Woodpecker in the silver birch tree in our back garden

January 2016

Subaru Impreza, Dacia Sandero Stepway and a Chaff Finch

Time for a Change

We decided this month that Susie's car, which is a Subaru Impreza, is getting old and that we should consider replacing it with a new car in the near future. We looked on the Internet, and visited a few car showrooms in Kings Lynn, before deciding that we liked the look of the new Dacia Sandero Stepway. Having decided what we liked we set out on the 16th January to visit the main dealer for Dacia, Wests Garage (KL) ltd. In Kings Lynn. Wandering around the forecourt we looked at several examples of this car and decided that yes, we liked the car but now we needed to test drive it just to make sure it was what Susie and I wanted. We arranged this with one of their salesmen, Robert, for the 22nd January and then went home. On the designated day, (22nd) we picked up the test drive car, the same model as we liked the look of, from the garage and Susie drove it to Swaffham, Downham Market and on other roads for about an hour. She said that yes, this was the car for her, so we ordered a new white one which will be delivered soon to the dealer and we can collect it from there. So we have now identified, tested and selected our new car which will be here next month. Oh happy days! **Update 2020:** I am pleased to say that our Dacia Sandero Stepway that we have had since February 2016 has been brilliant and we hope to be able to keep it for many more years to come!…

January 2016

Vets, weeding, walking the dogs and a robin in our garden

On the 29th January Susie, took Poppy to the vets at 9 am, to have a check-up. Poppy had been sick and off her food for the last two days. After checking her over, and giving her an injection, the vet said that she may have eaten something that was not good for her. He also, said that she should be fine once the injection gets to work, but to bring her back if the symptoms do not clear up in the next few days. While there Susie booked Poppy in next month to be spayed. Today, it was surprisingly sunny and quite warm for January, so when Susie got home from the vets, she busied herself with working outside in our garden. First she weeded our back garden rose bed, followed by all the other beds in our back garden. This, created three bags of plant waste, which she then put into our brown re-cycling bin, ready for it's collection next week. Having done all of the above by 2 pm, we decided to take the dogs for a long walk in Shouldham Warren which they loved…

January 2016

Back to my Writing

By the end of January I had completed the written drafts, editing and published two new books. That is the 9th and 10th books that I have had published to date. The books are called "Art Inspired by a Rainbow" and "Ibiza Island of Dreams". The first book, as the title suggests, showcases my latest artworks and watercolour paintings. The second book is a traveller's guide to the beautiful Mediterranean island of Ibiza in both words and artwork illustrations. In February I plan to finish working on a book called "Majorca Island in the Sun" and get it published by the end of the month. All of my books are now available on Amazon and from other good book retailers. **Update 2020:** My plan to update and re-publish all of my twenty paperback books as 3rd editions during April, May and June 2020 has move on at a pace and to-date (10th May) I have managed to complete the re-publication of Eleven 3rd & 4th Editions!…

February 2016

The Sleep Over - Ginny and Bertie

On Friday 5th February Ginny came to stay with us, with her dog Bertie, for a couple of days. It was her birthday on Saturday so when we got up she opened her presents before having a nice birthday breakfast meal. After spending some time recovering from our meal and looking at her presents we all took Charlie, Poppy and Bertie for a long walk in Shouldham Warren. The weather was cool and dry and the woods was busy with horse riders, cyclists and people walking their dogs. It was very enjoyable. The dogs were exhausted when we got back home. Leaving the dogs at home to rest and recover from their long walk/run Susie and I took Ginny for a celebration birthday lunch at a restaurant just outside Downham Market. It was great to see her and enjoy her and Bertie's company for a couple of days but it was soon time for them to go back home and for us to settle down for an evening by the TV with our dogs…

February 2016

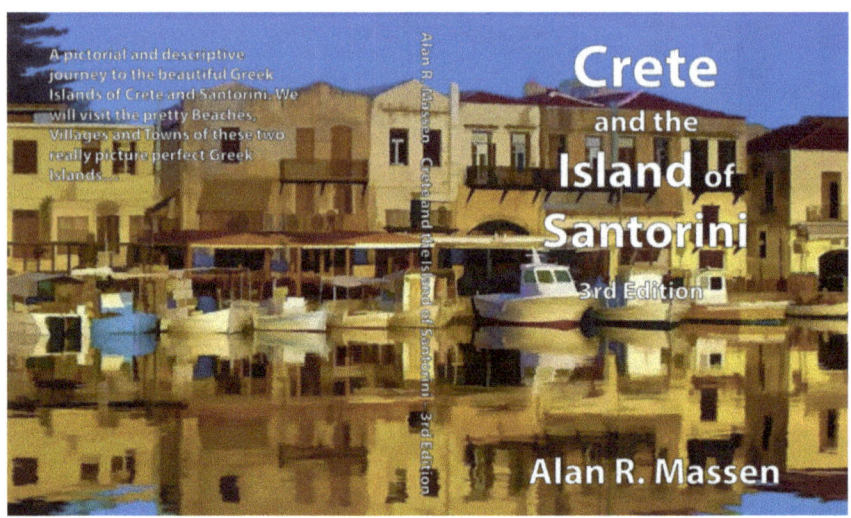

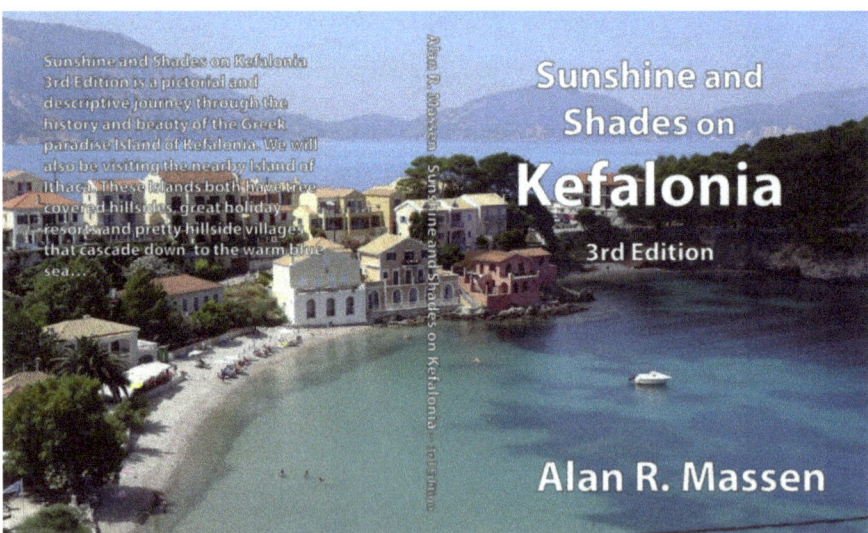

Back to my Writing

I heard from my publisher today that two more of my books are to be published this month. They are about the Spanish Island of Majorca and the Greek Island of Thassos. These will be available on Amazon and from other good book retailers soon. I will receive a dozen paperbacks of each soon. They will be the 11th and 12th books that I have had published to date. **Update 2020:** My plan to update and re-publish all of my twenty paperback books as 3rd and 4th Editions during April, May and June 2020 is still progressing at a pace…

February 2016

New for Old

On Wednesday 5th February Susie and I, after taking the dogs on a long walk first thing in the morning, settling the dogs down at home, left home at 10.30 am on a mission. We drove to Wests of Kings Lynn, a car dealership, to trade in our old car for a swanky new car. We had decided last month that it was time to change our car for a new model. Having completed the handover and paperwork it was time to collect the keys for our new car and drive it away for the first time. We were delighted with the performance and look of our gleaming new white Dasia. When we got home it was straight onto the Internet to order a set of internal car mats to protect the floors which arrived two days later and fitted perfectly. The only other job left to do was to install the grill between the back seats and the boot so the dogs can travel safely in their new transport. After this was done it was time to load the dogs into the back and take them on their first journey in our new family car. **Update 2020:** As I have already said we still have the car today and it is running very well…

February 2016

St Valentine's Day - Derbyshire Gemstones and Silver

On Sunday 14th February Susie and I exchanged presents and cards as a token of our love for each other. Today is traditionally the day when you do this in the UK. I gave Susie a pair of hallmarked silver and Blue John gemstone earring's. I was fascinated to learn that hallmarks are one of the original forms of customer protection. They were introduced into the UK over 700 years ago. A hallmark is a small marking on a gold, silver or platinum item and confirms that the product has been tested by an independent organisation (Assay Office) and conforms to the required standard of composition. There are only four Assay Offices in the UK, in London, Birmingham, Sheffield and Edinburgh. I also learnt, about the earrings that I gave Susie, that the Blue John used in them, is now a very rare and mysterious semi-precious gemstone only mined around the Peak District village of Castleton, Derbyshire. We stayed at Edale very near Castleton for a week last October and Susie mentioned then that she would like to have some of these gemstones so she was well pleased that I had remembered this and she now had some. PS Susie baked me the above steak and kidney pie for us to eat on the day.
Update Friday February 14th 2020: Susie received more precious Blue John gemstones for Valentines Day from me this year. This year I gave her a silver pendant in a heart shape that looked a bit like lucky shamrock and each segment (3) contained a Blue John gemstone in it. She loved it!…

February 2016

Snow on Snow

When we got up on Monday 15th February everywhere was white. It had snowed over night for the first time this year and everything looked magical. The dogs were very excited and after being fed and Susie had cleared the car of snow and warmed it up we set off for Shouldham Warren. We wrapped up warm and after arriving at the woods car park we wandered into the snow capped trees. Us and the dogs loved walking (us) and running (them) through the snow and seeing all the trees and grass covered in snow which glistened in the bright morning sunshine. We spent about two hours out and arrived back home again at about 11 am and within an hour the snow had all melted and you would not have thought that just a short time ago everything was as white as snow!. **Update 2020:** The strange things is that since 2016 we have virtually had little or no snow every year since. This year 2020 we have had just a fine sprinkling on two days only. Strange but true!…

February 2016

Out and About

It is now that time of year to start planning for the new season in our garden so on Friday 19th February Susie and I decided to go and see what bedding plants, bulbs and tubers Dobbies had available and at what cost. We went after we had finished our weekly shopping at Tesco's. They had a good selection but seemed rather expensive so on the way home we decided to call into Downham Country Store to see what they had. They had a better priced selection of summer bulbs and tubers so we selected fourteen packs of these. On the way to the till we noticed a pair of outside fuchsia coloured plastic chairs on half-price sale. These also had to come home with us. When we got home we decided to go on line and order some bedding plants from Van Meuwen. After looking on line we selected the following plants: 24 Gazania "Stars in strips", 24 Petunia "mixed", 5 Lantana "lucky", 24 Geranium "mixed", 72 Summer bedding plants "mixed" and 10 Dahlia "Unwin mix". So now we are prepared for the new season with only trailing plants, Lobelia and marigolds left to get. So our trip out and about the garden centres and on line will hopefully ensure a colourful and blooming summer again in our garden this year. **Update 2020:** Every year we re-new our garden flowers and since 2017 we have gone to Didlington Nurseries for most of our bedding and pot plants as they have a good selection at very reasonable prices. Yesterday (18th May) we completed putting all of this years purchases into our garden pots and beds. All we have to do know is to feed them, deadhead them and watch them grow.

Big Day for a Very Brave Girl

At 8.30 am on Wednesday 24th February Susie took Poppy to the vets to be spayed. We had decided that after getting Charlie done last year it was now time for Poppy to be done! Charlie stayed at home with me. We were both nervous and hoped that all went well. Susie came home alone and then it was just a question of us waiting until 2 pm to phone the vets to see how her operation had gone. Rather than sit around we took Charlie to Shouldham Warren for a long walk and to take all our minds of worrying about Poppy. At the appointed hour of 2 pm Susie phone the vets to be told that all had gone well and Poppy could be picked up at 4 pm. We were all relieved. When Susie got home at 4.30 pm, with a very sorry for herself Poppy, who immediately went and laid down quietly on our couch in the lounge. She did manage to eat something for her tea and much to our relief she slept through the night. The next day she continued to gradually improve. She will need to be kept on the lead when outside for the next ten days. We were both very proud of how she had coped with her major surgery and looked forward to when she is back to her old charging around self again…

March 2016

Making the Cut(s)

To celebrate the beginning of a new month, I decided to charge up the hedge cutter, and finish off the trimming of all of our garden hedges, front and back, that I started last autumn, to make sure they looked tidy, for the new season ahead. So on Tuesday 1st March I took some pain killers to suppress any pain I may get from my poorly right knee. Collected the gear and started in on the front hedge. My right knee, did not like getting up and down off the stool, that I was using to reach the top of the hedge, very much. The battery used in the hedge cutter did not hold its charge very long and discharged after just half an hour. The next few days stayed dry and sunny but cold and although it took me three more days to complete the cutting of all of our garden hedges. **Update 2020:** Obviously this is a task that is required regularly to keep the hedging looking at its best and not get to high or overgrown. I like doing it but with my knees as they are often I have to ask Susie for help. I am pleased to say that I have replaced my battery operated hedge trimmer with one that is powered from the mains electricity so I can cut as much as my knees can stand without having to recharge my battery! This year in February 2020 the amount of hedge cutting that we need to do has now been reduced by 33%. Our next door neighbour has removed the hedge from the right had side of our garden and replaced it with a six foot high wooden fence. We are both please and relieved!…

March 2016

I am updating this Book right NOW!…

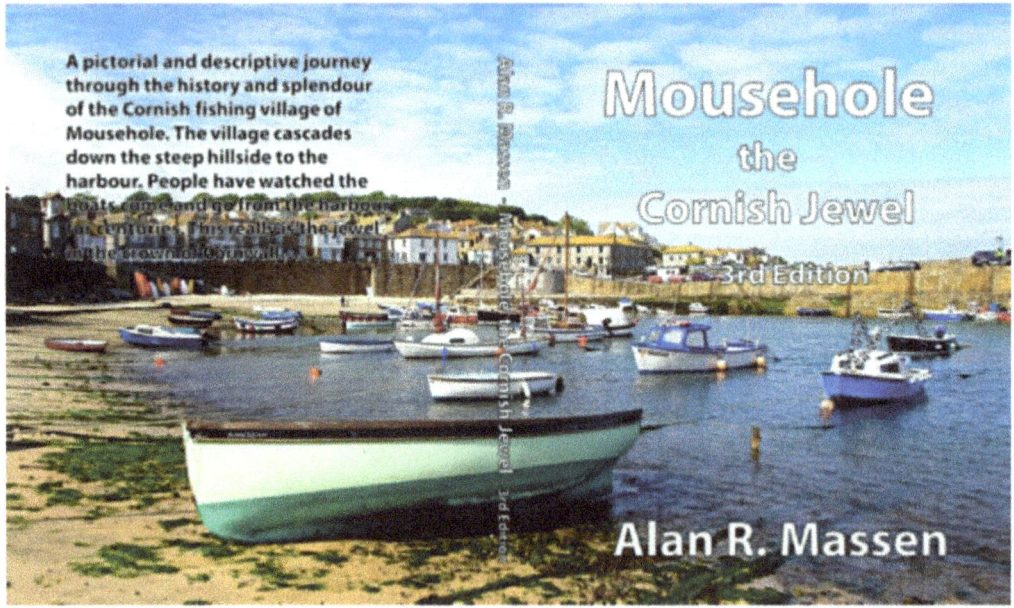

Back to my Writing - Multi-Tasking

This March I have continued to write, not just on this book, but I have started writing the draft for my next book which will be called "England the Country of my Birth". **Update 2020:** My plan to update and re-publish all of my twenty paperback books as 3rd & 4th Editions during April, May and June 2020 is still progressing nicely and to-date (27th May) I have completed the re-publication of eleven of my 3rd & 4th Edition Books!…

March 2016

…Wine Making

Our Poppy…

So Far So Good!

On Sunday the 6th March we started another batch of our home made wine. I then weighed myself and found that I have now managed to lose more than two stones to-date. I started at 118 KG and I am now down to 105 KG. Susie has also managed to lose one stone since we started our diet together on January 1st this year. I am also well chuffed that since we stopped smoking last November Susie and I have managed to stay off the weed. We both feel so much better for doing so. I am now on target of being a non-smoker with a weight below 100 KG in the next few weeks/months. When achieved, it will mean that I can return to see my surgeon Mr. James Jeffery to arrange for me to go into hospital to get my right knee replacement operation done. It is amazing to think that it is almost one year since I had my left total knee replacement operation done on the 1st April 2015. My left knee is now great so I hope that the same will be true when I have my right knee done. On Monday Poppy, our female dog, went to the vets to be sterilised and by the end of the week I am pleased to say she was fully recovered and charging around like a fool, much like she usually does…

March 2016

Last years wild flower bed in our garden

The First Cut

On Thursday 10th March I managed to give our back lawn its first cut of the year while Susie weeded all our flower beds in the back garden. After these tasks were done, we were able to sit up on the decking with the dogs, as it was very sunny and quite warm today. As we enjoyed a coffee (you should always find time for a coffee) we discussed what plants, bulbs, tubers and seeds we would put where this year. We decided that we would, once again, this year, wild flower seed the silver birch bed using all the saved seeds we harvested from last year's successful wild flowers. The plug plants that we have ordered, will all be planted in the pots and flower beds in the garden and patio and in the front and back garden when they arrive. As the weather was kind Susie then seeded the wild seed mix into the silver birch bed while I completed the spring plant pruning tasks in the garden. While we were doing these jobs Susie noticed that the blue tits were starting to use the nesting boxes that we have put up for them on the house and shed. So who knows soon we could be watching new life come into our garden. **Update 2020:** This year I made the first cut to our lawn on the 23rd February. This was mainly because of the very mild winter and early spring sunshine but also dare I say it to global warming. We should all be very afraid!!!

March 2016

The Kiss, Wild Foxgloves in Shouldham Warren, The Front of our House and Charlie and Poppy in our Garden

A new sign is born

On Monday 14th March, Kevin, our window cleaner came and cleaned all our windows which was great. It was nice to see him again and catch up on all his news. Last winter our house sign, in the front garden, was blown down and was broken. Whilst out shopping last week we found a suitable blank piece of metal. Later that day, Susie, painted a new house sign, for us, on it. When it was dry she asked me to put it up in our front garden. After fixing it to a metal post we looked for a suitable location for displaying it so it could be easily seen from the road. We found an ideal spot in the middle of our front grass bank bed. I erected the sign and we both agreed it looked great. Susie then seeded around the sign with some marigold seeds so it will not only tell others what our house name is but will also look pretty. **Update 2020:** Although the grass bank was replaced by the three tiered graveled steps (see above) in 2019 we retained the house sign and will find an alternative place to display it real soon…

March 2016

Planting the Tubers and Bulbs

As the weather was good on Friday 25th March, I decided to spend the day, working in the garden, planting out the summer flowering tubers and bulbs, that we have purchased for this year's garden beds and pots. I reviewed what we had, where I would be planting them and wrote some plant labels to place in the pots or garden beds when I planted them. Susie, went off to walk the dogs while I made a start. It took me several hours to complete the work but I was well pleased to have completed this vital spring job. I planted out the following tubers and bulbs that we hope will grow and give us a nice show of colour this summer: **POTS:** 2 hardy Gloxinia – 10 hardy Nymph Gladioli – 25 Peacock Orchids – 2 Ismene Festalis – 10 Tigridia – 1 Dahlia Orange – 2 Dahlia Pompon – 13 Dahlia Unwin – 20 Allium Moly – **GARDEN BEDS:** 10 Gladioli Atom – 20 Lintris Spicata – 10 Oxalis – 20 Anemone – 15 Dutch Iris – 4 Lilies Asiatic. When they produce flowers later this year they will be used by Susie as cut flowers in our house. After planting all of the above tubers and bulbs all we could do now was to sit back and wait for nature to take its course…

March 2016

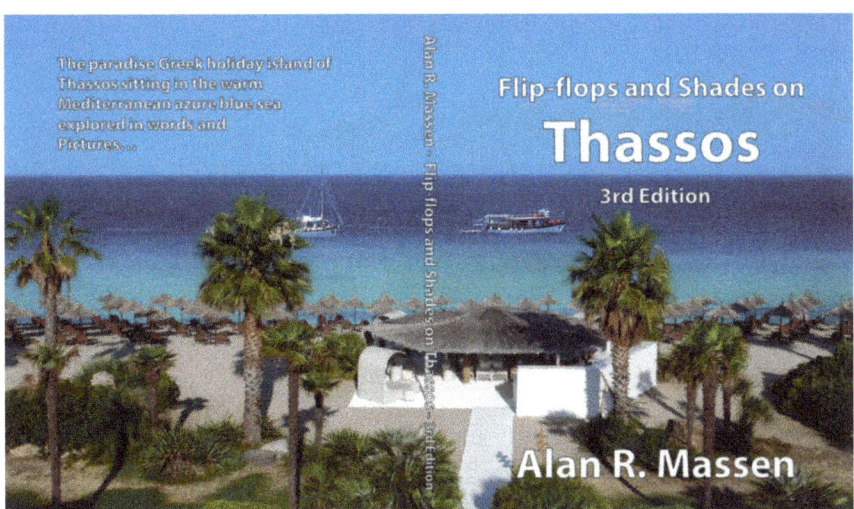

More Books

By the end of March, I had nearly finished my book called "England the Country of my Birth" and have also started writing the drafts of two more books that are called "Sunshine and Shades on Kefalonia and Shades and Flip-flops on Zakynthos". These should keep me busy until the gardening season begins for real in late April. **Update 2020:** My plan to update and re-publish all of my twenty paperback books as 3rd & 4th Editions during April, May and June of 2020 is still progressing nicely…

March 2016

Mum, Johnny and her dog Ellie (who sadly died in 2016) and Mum and Alan

Mums Coming!

On Sunday 27th March Susie drove up to Sheffield to pick up her Mum to bring her back to stay at ours for the next few days or maybe even for a week or more. She drove back with her Mum on Easter Monday and not wishing to meet my mothering-in-law scruffy I looked through my wardrobe for something sensible to wear! As I have lost more than two stone in the last few weeks I can now fit into all the clothes that, I bought in the past, with much optimism, only to find that I could not do them up when I got them home. You know how it is. Us men, being too lazy to try them on in the shop. So many of them have sat in my wardrobe and draws for years. With a sense of excitement I got started by trying some of my un-worn trousers on and found to my delight that I could now do them up easily. I selected a pair of cotton trousers that I have had since 2008 and never worn and a white shirt that I have had since 2014 and never worn. I was then able to present myself smartly, to Mum when she arrived, in my new (old) clothes that I have now grown down into!…

April 2016

April in Norfolk

Fools Rush In!

April 1st in England is the traditional day for people to play practical jokes on their friends and relations but I managed to contain myself and did not make any mischief, on the day, in fact as Susie's Mum Ann was still with us we all went out to Hunstanton for the day. It was a lovely day and after taking light refreshments in Old Hunstanton we journeyed home via the Moat nursery so I could buy some more plants for our garden. Ann (Susie's Mum) also got herself a new plant so we were all very pleased. Susie drove her Mum back to Sheffield on Sunday 3rd April. It was really lovely to have her to stay for a week and hopefully she will come again in the summer. While Susie was away the dogs and I enjoyed the spring sunshine in our back garden and I cut the lawn. When she got home at about 4 pm we all stayed in the garden, on the decking, for another hour or so having nibbles and drinks (just us, the dogs had a small dog biscuit each!)…

April 2016

Back to the Baking

Once again, this month (April 2016), Susie has been busy baking and has made us some lovely cup cakes and a red onion tarte tatin (see above).

Baking in 2020

Update 2020: Since 2016 Susie has continued to bake regularly and only this week 01.03.2020 she has produced the wonderful Pear and Almond pie that you see above. I have been so lucky over the last four years to have had the opportunity to sample such delights as these on a regular basis so to Susie I say thank you very much and keep on baking…

April 2016

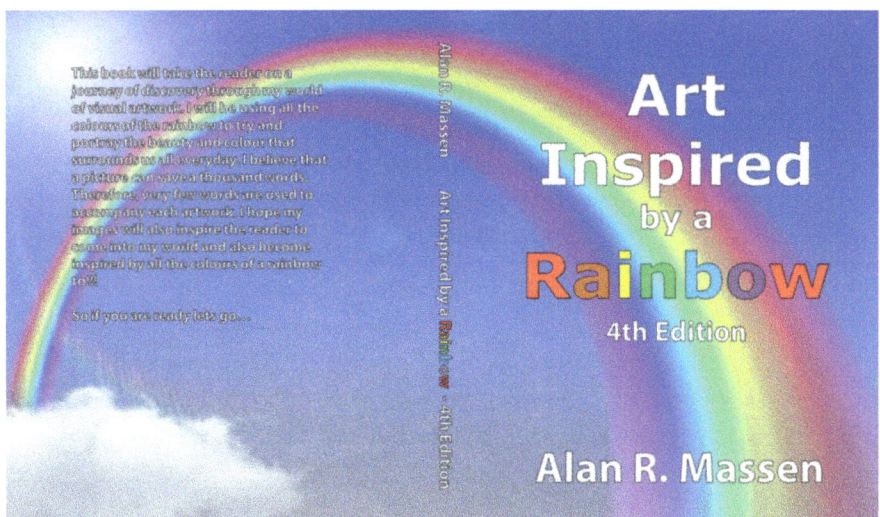

Back to the Writing

This month I have started doing the research and the designing of the book covers for two more books which are entitled: "Crete and the Island of Santorini" and "Cyprus the Pyramids and the Holy Land". **Update 2020:** My plan to update and re-publish all of my twenty paperback books as 3rd & 4th Editions during April, May and June of 2020 is nearly done and to-date (15th June) I have completed the re-publication of eighteen 3rd & 4th Editions of my books…

April 2016

Lynn, Andy with the late Franky and my latest 2020 Skiathos book

Our friends both home and abroad

On Sunday 10th April something stirred in the skies above Norfolk! Today I put my shorts on for the first time this year because it was very sunny and quite warm today. Susie and I sat up on the decking with the dogs when all of a sudden Susie said : Hey look there! Soaring in the sky above us was three swallows. How great. The swallows have returned so now we can relax as summer is truly here at last. On Friday 15th April our friends Andy and Lynn with their dog Franky came to stay with us for a couple of days (Franky sadly died in February 2020). They live near Sheffield and it was really great to see them once more. We enjoyed, for dinner, one of Susie's classic three course Greek meals which she had cooked from recipes in the Rick Stein Venice to Istanbul cookery book. It was magnificent. Well done Susie and thank you Rick. In the morning Susie took our dogs along with them and Franky for a walk in Shouldham Warren before breakfast. Our friends left at around lunchtime to make the journey back home. Before they left I asked them to do us a favour. Unlike us, they are once more, in June, holidaying at the Troulos Bay Hotel on Skiathos. So I asked them if they would kindly take some copies of my recently published book, featuring the paradise island of Skiathos, and give them to our Greek friends who live and work on Skiathos. They agreed to do this for me and we hope that we to will be going back to Skiathos once more very soon. **Update 2020:** Unfortunately, largely due to my very poorly knees and financial constraints, we have not been able, as yet, to return to our beloved Troulos Bay Hotel on Skiathos however, every year since 2016 Andy and Lynn have been kind enough to take a copy of one of my books to give to our Skiathan friends as a gift from us. We thank Andy and Lynn very much and we hope to do the same this year when we will send them a copy of our latest Skiathos book published in 2020…

April 2016

Back to my Studio

Artworks from my studio: Cat called Sam, Rainbow Warrior and George the Zebra. April has been very wet this year so I have had more time to paint. **Update 2018:** Talking about April showers in 2018 we actually had a wet room built onto our downstairs sun room.

The Wet Room!

Update 2020: Because of the problems I have climbing stairs and my poor general mobility we decided in 2018 to plan ahead and have a toilet and shower (wet room)built on the ground floor of our house. The wet room was built by Suiter Construction Limited from May to July 2018 and a great job they made of it. Thank you Tom. Now two years on we use the wet room every day and should I not be able to climb the wooded stairs to bed in the future then I can sleep in the sun room and use our new downstairs wet room as an on suite! A good plan or what!…

April 2016

Back to our Garden

By late April all of the plug plants (72 plants in total) that we had nurtured in our sunroom were ready to be hardened off (which means putting them outside during the day but bring them back inside at night to protect them from the cold). On Thursday 28th April it was time to do the same thing with the plants we have grown on from plug plants (96 plants) in our greenhouse. Once we have hardened all these plants off, which will take about ten days, dependent on the weather, we will plant them either into pots or into the flower beds in our front or back garden hoping for a great summer of colour. Once this task is completed all we will have to do, during the rest of the season, is to feed, water, dead head and keep the grass mowed. This should leave us plenty of time to sit on our patio or decking and enjoy watching the swallows soaring in the sky, while having, a few cold drinks, some nice meals and/or just to enjoy natures feast of colour, sights and sounds. **Update 2020:** Every year since 2016 we have been able to repeat the above sequence of life by planting the summer bedding plants, watching the swallows swoop and listening to the birds singing in our garden whilst enjoying a cold beer, a Cuba Libre and/or a glass or two of wine. Some would say we are lucky but I would say that we are just enjoying the fruits of our hard won labours!…

April 2016

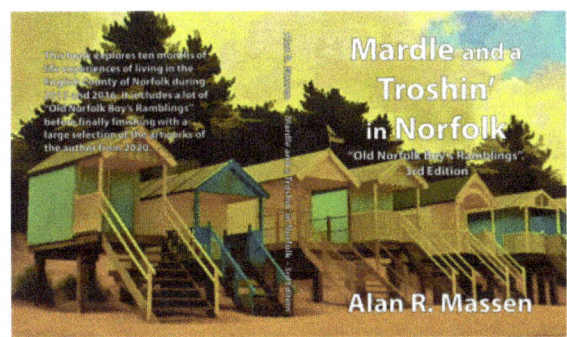
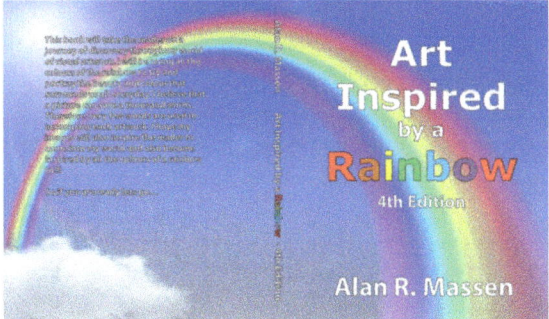

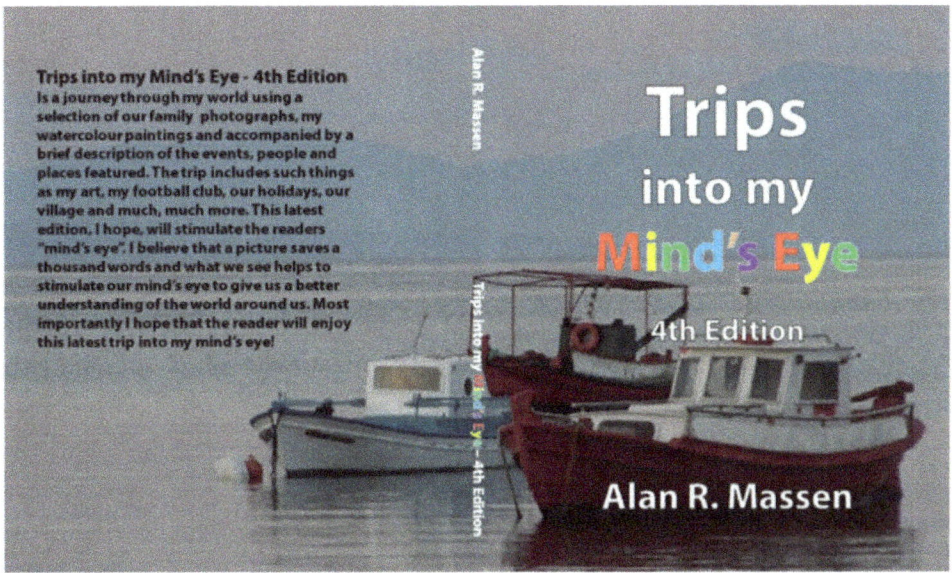

In the end it is back to my writing

Now that we are at the end of April I have started doing the research and designing of the book covers for two new books which will be entitled: "Corfu and Mainland Greece" and "Trips into my Mind's Eye". I hope to publish these in May 2016. **Update 2020:** My plan to update and re-publish all of my twenty paperback books as 3rd & 4th Editions during April, May and June of 2019 has been a resounding success and to-date (28th June) I have completed my re-publication of all twenty of my books and I have even managed to complete and re-publish my "Trips into my Mind's Eye" in a 4th Edition! As we also come to the end of our ten months together, we will, in the next, but last, chapter, as is our want and keep right on the road to a **Mardling and a Troshin' to the End…**

Mardling and a Troshin' to the End

I think that it is amazing, looking back, just how much has happened to me and around me in the last ten months. I have recovered from the major surgery that I had last April to replace my left knee, I have written and had published ten books, produced numerous artworks and paintings, missed out on a foreign holiday for the first time for many years, sold my car, given up driving, stopped smoking completely, lost more than fourteen kilograms of weight, started gardening again and even more strange I have begun to enjoy reading poetry once more after so many years. The poem that sums up, for me, how proud I am to be a Norwich boy is the one written by John Kett in our own unique Norfolk language:

A Fine City - By John Kett

Dew yew come wi' me; come yew up the hill t'the Heath, An' look over the gorse, an' right down t'the city beneath. See that gret spire, an' the castle a-standin' so square, The towers o' the chaaches, an chimmaleys everawhere. Tha's Norridge.

See them gret buildin's, so new; all them winders t'clean; An' plenty o' patches where trees show a nice bit o' green. An' look at them thousands o' hooms, an' ar own City Hall; An' p'raps see a bit o' the river what run trew it all. Tha's Norridge.

There's old, an' there's new, an' there's changes what may seem a shame; But that oon't dew, y'know, fer a plaace t'stay allus the same. Tha's Norridge, bor, all on'it – ah, an I reckon tha's fine! My haart an' I'm proud on' it; somehow, that fare t'be mine – My Norridge.

As John Kett once said -Tha's a Rum'un, Bor!

I have even attempted to write some poetry myself. Now it is time to return back to my roots. In this chapter we explore Norfolk, its people, my favourite poems and the strange way in which we communicate (the Norfolk dialect) before finishing with some artwork in the last chapter…

Mardling and a Troshin' to the End

The Norfolk motto: ' Do Different.'

An Old Norfolk saying: The prevailing wind in Norfolk is onshore; this explains why Norfolk men invariably speak with their mouths closed. Norfolk is cut off on three sides by the North Sea and on the fourth by British Rail.

Words of Wisdom about Norfolk

I am a Norfolk man and Glory in being so (by my hero Horatio Nelson).

If the rest of Britain sank beneath the waves, and Norfolk was left alone, islanded in the turmoil of the seas, it would, I think, survive without too much trouble. Norfolk has always stood alone and aloof from the rest of England (by James Wentworth Day).

In the Middle Ages and well on into the eighteenth century, when roads were bad, it was easier to travel by sea from Norfolk to the continent of Europe than to penetrate the Midlands or to visit London. The result of this isolation has been that Norfolk people have become self-reliant, self-supporting and inclined to treat strangers with caution (by Bernard E. Dorman).

A whispering and watery Norfolk sound telling of all the moonlit reeds around (by John Betjeman).

Norfolk: In that country of luminous landscapes and wide horizons where the wind runs in the reeds and the slow rivers flow to our cold sea, a man may still sense and live something of the life of the older England which was uninhibited, free and natural (by Alan Savory, A Norfolk Fowler)…

Mardling and a Troshin' to the End

Getting Old in Norfolk

When I retired in 2008 I spent much of my time, in good weather, gardening in our Norfolk garden. I was encouraged by my wife Susie to keep a daily diary. As things occurred I would note them down. In bad weather, I also continued my other passion of watercolour painting. When I had filled several notebooks with my ramblings on our garden Susie suggested that I should use these to write a gardening book. This started me on the road to becoming a published author of not just gardening books but of art books, history and travel books. In the last year, 2016, I have re-discovered my love of poetry. Whilst reading John Kett's book "Tha's a Rum'un, Bor! I found one of his poems that captured, for me, what gardening is often about!

My Garden - By the late John Kett (a good old Norfolk boy)

All summer long my neerbours' garden grow
Ahid o' mine. Their peas an' beans stand high
Compared wi' my lot, though I wholly try;
An' all their flar-beds maake a lovela show.

That seem as though, whenever I sow seeds
They fare t'come up slow, or not a'tall.
An' them there hollahocks agin that wall
In't haalf as big as them untidy weeds.

But I'll say one thing, bor, an' that in't tew-
Now Winter's come, an' that ole North wind blow,
My garden's buried und'ra foot o' snow…
That look like all the others now, that dew!

Many of my readers may not be able to fully understand the Norfolk dialect used in the poem above BUT I hope you will be able to get the typical Norfolk humour of the last two lines…

Mardling and a Troshin' to the End

The Strange Way we Speak in Norfolk
Some examples of weird Norfolk words by Arthur H. Patterson

Bor, I never cood arn much money, no matter how 'ard I try'd; but never wor short o' dumplins or a good owd eel well fry'd. Bor, I ha' found owd Norfolk frindly, an' I married a Norfolk gal, an' when I cum off o' the marshes, I've found her a good owd pal. Law! I ha' lived wi' monkeys, and worked where the lions roar, but I longed tu heer t' owd curlews "Whaup" front o' th' houseboat door. So I drifted back tu owd Norfolk, and heer I intend tu 'bide; for the bards, an' t' fishes, an' people of Norfolk, air all my pride. When Broadland is left for Jordan, and Charon cum over th' styx, du delve a deep hole in owd Norfolk whose sile wi' my ashes shell mix.

Ole Mr Blanchflower Wot Allus Do the 'nnouncements
At the Troshin' Fair Tell 'em Wot's On:

Fust we hev on an expedition of thatchin' wot include layin' and tyin' and cross-hatchin', follered at two by a tork on eel catchin'. Then we hev the W.I. singin' for yew thar own varsion of Jerusalem, wot's bran new (Tho' Mrs Black int har cos she's orf with the flu). At three we'll be a hevin' the best tastin' caerke (Wot, this yar, 'll be judged by the Reverend Blake), Then the Broadshire Battle Grup—arter a short break will be a doin' thar Hastin's (1066). Larst we hev the Thrapston Morris Men and thar sticks, accompanied on harmonicals by Sid Hicks.

Please have a stab at translating the above examples of the way we people of Norfolk talk but I will understand it if readers want to just move on and read, in English, about a great Norfolk boy who became a national British hero for valour…

Mardling and a Troshin' to the End

A Norfolk lament to Lord Nelson - A Great Norfolk Hero

Echoes of War – By William Riviere

In Norfolk the freezing wind which roared in the trees around Paston church battered all the flint churches which stood parish after parish along the coast of muddy cliffs and salt marshes and shingle foreshores, frenzied to a St Vitus' dance the blizzard-stunted sycamores and oaks and thorns. In the region of windmills, the storm shrieked in their rusting turning gears, shook their groaning spars. The anchorage at Brancaster was protected by the island of Scolt Head, but even inshore before the village the white waves reared awesomely around the moored fishing-smacks.

All afternoon in the relative hush of low tide the men had checked their warps. They had overhauled mooring-chains, they had laid out kedge-anchors. They had rowed ashore in their cockling scows. Now at high water their smacks were exposed to the undiminished force of the gale; they chucked their tethered heads like frightened horses; they shuddered under the blows of the breaking seas. At Burnham where Horatio Nelson had learned to sail, at Wells where he had watched luggers loading and unloading, the black tide foamed up the creeks, it flooded the marshes of sea-lavender and marram grass, it stormed against the sea-walls.

Off Stiffkey, where at low tide in summer the Lammas family liked to walk their dogs on the revealed sand-banks, by nightfall the harbour bar was a maelstrom thirty foot deep, the tide had advanced two miles inshore, had whelmed the samphire flats and the river mouth and the mussel beds in one navigable welter of crossing pale crest and dark troughs. At Mundesley, where Charles Lammas' father Roland had lived and had his studio at Cliff House, winter by winter yards of what had been his rose garden and tennis court and vegetable garden had been lost to the North Sea…

Mardling and a Troshin' to the End

A Famous Norfolk Song

Hey Yew Gotta Loight Boy? by Allan Smethurst the Norfolk Singing Postman

I had a gal, a rare nice gal, down in Wroxham way, she were whooly nice ter me in the ole school days. She would smile all the while, but Daddy dint know all what she used ter say ter me behind the garden wall. 'Hev yew gotta loight, boy? hev yew gotta loight, boy?' Molly Windley, she smook like a chimley, but she's my little nicoteen gal.

Then one day, she went away, I dunt see har no more, till by chance, I see har down along th' Mundesley shore. She wuz there, twice as fair, would she now be trew? So when she see me passin' by she say 'I'm glad thass yew, hev yew gotta loight, boy? hev yew gotta loight?' Molly Windley, she smook like a chimley, but she's my little nicoteen gal.

Now yew'll see har an' me never more t'part, we would wander hand in hand tergether in the dark. Then one night I held har tight in th' ole back yard, But when I tried to hold har close, she say 'Now hold yew hard! Hev yew gotta loight, boy? hev yew gotta loight? Molly Windley, she smook like a chimley, but she's my little nicoteen gal.

By and by we decide on th' weddin' day, so we toddle orff ter chatch ter hear the preacher say: 'Do yew now tearke this vow ter honour all the time?' Afore I had th'chance ter stop har, she begin ter pine: Hev yew gotta loight, boy? hev yew gotta loight? Molly Windley, she smook like a chimley, but she's my little nicoteen gal.

Now the doctor tell me a Daddy I will be, So when I arsk him 'Woss th' score?' he say 'There's only three' so, here I go, cheerioo, ter see how she do fare, I know what she will say ter me as soon as I git there: Hev yew gotta loight, boy? hev yew gotta loight? Molly Windley, she smook like a chimley, but she's my little nicoteen gal…

Mardling and a Troshin' to the End

The Norfolk Legend of the Swaffham Tinker by Anon

John Chapman was a tinker who lived in Swaffham Town, one night he dreamed a voice did say if you win renown, then he must go to London Bridge, and there the voice did cry he'd find a man to tell him where wondrous treasure lies. So Chapman came to London Bridge, but no man did he see, till a Butcher's boy came whistling by, so careless and so free; As he passed by he did let fall a sheep's head on the ground, and Chapman said to a passer-by, 'Oh see what I have found.

The man he said that all was well, the sheep's head he'd restore, but first good friends, as he seem tired, pray tell me now some more. What brought you up to London to seek the city wide? Said John, 'A dream brought me to London - a fool's game I have tried.' Yes, friend you are most foolish, to leave your home like this, to wander up to London, for dreams of fancied bliss, where no man cares for others, save as they serve their plan, to rob and slay each other, and best their fellow man.

Now hark to me, a month ago, while sleeping in my chair, I thought I heard some church bells chiming clearly in the air, the voices hovered o'er me, that seemed to me to say, neath the Eastern door of Swaffham Church great buried treasure lay. I dreamed I had found a coffer, of many guineas bright, then I searched again for thirty rods, till there came into sight a heavy moss-grown arch of stone, and after that a cross, then I deeper dug for others that lay like useless dross.

He who jested did not notice the change in Chapman's eye, nor heeded he the tremor, his dog Jasper did decry. Through common, lane and byway, homeward he quickly sped, when money failed he tinkered, to earn his daily bread. A comely widow where he halted offered heart, and home, and barn and you who smile and read this, therein can see no harm, but Chapman never tarried, his heart was not his own, he knew his wife and children waited for him at home…

Mardling and a Troshin' to the End

The Norfolk Legend of the Swaffham Tinker by Anon

At length he reached his cottage door, to hear his good wife's cry, 'God bring me back my husband to bless me ere I die.' But still he never lingered save to light his lantern at the fire, and hurried through the churchyard till at last he reached the spire.

There was the arch stone surely, and lifting proved the key, for below the found the shining gold of wondrous mystery. He filled his leather apron quite full ten times or more, and then with superhuman strength the coffer home he bore.

He cleaned it bright and shining, and on the coming day there passed two men of learning, 'Why look you here,' said they; 'Of what is this inscription - 'Beneath me you will find, another one containing much treasure of the same kind.

This is an ancient coffer from Norman times methinks, the tinker sees no value save to buy him meat and drink. Now all who read this legend, let it be true or not, can learn a weighty lesson that must not be forgot…

Mardling and a Troshin' to the End

Norfolk the Land of the Turkey – By Marshall

Norfolk is celebrated, and justly, for its turkeys. The species is large; their flesh, nevertheless, fine; and the number reared greater than that produced in any other district of equal extent; owing, perhaps, to one circumstance. It is understood, in general, that, to rear turkeys with success, it is necessary that a male bird should be kept upon the spot, for the same purpose that a gander, a drake, or a male fowl is kept; namely to impregnate the eggs individually. This deters not only cottagers, who are afraid of the expense of keeping a gluttonous turkey-cock, the year round, but many farmers, who dislike the noise and trouble-some-ness of these animals from breeding turkeys. But the good housewives of this country know that a daily intercourse is unnecessary; and that, if the female be sent to a neighbouring male previous to the season of exclusion, one act of impregnation is sufficient for one brood. Thus relieved from the expense and disagreeableness of keeping a male bird, most little farmers, and many cottagers, rear turkeys. This accounts for the number; and the species, and the food they are fatted with (which I believe, is wholly buck) account for their superior size and quality. With respect to geese, ducks and fowls of this country, nothing is noticeable; except that they are, in general below common size, and that it is a practice to put young goslings upon green wheat: a piece of housewifery which perhaps is peculiars to the country. Poultry of every species are sold, in the markets, ready picked and skewered fit for the spit; and are, in general, so well fatted and dressed up in such neatness and delicacy, as she the Norfolk housewives to be mistresses in the art of managing poultry…

Mardling and a Troshin' to the End

Norfolk the Land of the Reed Cutter by W. A. Dutt

In winter, one of the most familiar sights in Broadland is a reed-cutter at work on a Broad or by the riverside. For the reed-cutter's harvest is a winter one, beginning about Christmas, when the blade is off the reeds, and lasting until March or April, when the appearance of the 'colts' or young reeds puts a stop to the cutting. Eel-catchers, marsh-men, mill-men, and the men who sail the cruising yachts, take part in this belated harvest, which comes at a time when there is little else for them to do in the daytime, and only wild fowl to be watched for at dusk and dawn. Scythe are used in cutting the reeds, and the cutter works either in a wide, flat bottomed marsh boat, or on a plank projecting from a boat or laid flat in a cleared space among the reeds. If, however, the reeds grow in shallow water, the men put on wading-boots and work in the water. The cut reeds are laid in the boat or where they are to be stacked. There they are tied in bundles or 'shooves', five of which are supposed to have an aggregate circumference of six feet, and they are sold by the fathom, a fathom of reeds being five 'shooves'. They are used for various purposes, such as supporting builders' plaster work, thatching cottages, park lodges, and ornamental boat-houses, and screening young shrubs and fruit trees; but the demand for them has decreased considerably since the days when there were 'scythe rights' on the reed fens and the reeds were carefully cultivated. But there are still many hundred acres of reeds in Broadland, and the cutting of them means a welcome addition to many scanty incomes. It can hardly now be called a profitable business. Still, there are a few men who cut and dry the reed…

Mardling and a Troshin' to the End

An Old Norfolk Boy's (ME) Favourite Poems

Snow - Poem by Walter de la Mare:

No breath of wind, No gleam of sun. Still the white snow whirls softly down Twig and bough and blade and thorn all in an icy Quiet, forlorn. Whispering, rustling, Through the air On sill and stone, Roof, - everywhere, It heaps its powdery Crystal flakes, Of every tree A mountain makes; Til pale and faint At shut of day Stoops from the West One wint'ry ray, and, feathered in fire where ghosts the moon, A robin shrills His lonely tune.

In Flanders Fields – Poem by John McCrae:

In Flanders fields the poppies blow between the crosses, row on row, that mark our places, and in the sky the larks, still bravely singing, fly scares heard amid the guns below. We are the dead, short days ago we lived, felt dawn, saw sunset glow, loved and were loved, and now we lie in Flanders fields. Take up our quarrel with the foe, to you from failing hands we throw the torch, be yours to hold it high. If ye break faith with us who die we shall not sleep, though poppies grow in Flanders fields.

Vinegar – Poem by Roger McGough:

Sometimes I feel like a priest in a fish & chip queue, quietly thinking as the vinegar runs through, how nice it would be to buy supper for two…

Mardling and a Troshin' to the End

The Night Mail – Poem by W.H.Auden

This is the night mail crossing the border, bringing the cheque and the postal order, letters for the rich, letters for the poor, the shop at the corner, the girl next door. Pulling up Beattock, a steady climb, the Gradient's against her, but she's on time. Past cotton-grass and moorland boulder, shoveling white steam over her shoulder, snorting noisily, she passes silent miles of wind bent grasses. Birds turn their heads as she approaches, Stare from bushes at her blank-faced coaches. Sheep-dogs cannot turn her courses, they slumber on with paws across. In the farm she passes no one wakes, but a jug in a bedroom gently shakes. Dawn freshens, her climb is done, down towards Glasgow she descends, towards the steam tugs yelping down a glade of cranes, towards the fields of apparatus, the furnaces set on the dark plain like gigantic chessmen.

All Scotland waits for her. In dark glens, beside pale-green lochs, men long for news. Letters of thanks, letters from banks, letters of joy from girl and boy, receipted bills and invitations to inspect new stock or to visit relations, and applications for situations, and timid lovers' declarations, and gossip, gossip from all the nations, news circumstantial, news financial, letters with holiday snaps to enlarge in, letters with faces scrawled on the margins, letters from uncles, cousins and aunts, letters to Scotland from the South of France, letters of condolence to highlands and lowlands, written on paper of every hue, the pink, the violet, the white and the blue, the chatty, the catty, the boring, the adoring, the cold and official and the heart's outpouring, clever, stupid, short and long, the typed and the printed and the spelt all wrong.

Thousands are still asleep, dreaming of terrifying monsters or a friendly tea beside the band in Cranston's or Crawford's, asleep in working Glasgow, asleep in well-set Edinburgh, asleep in granite Aberdeen, they continue their dreams, but shall wake soon and hope for letters, and none will hear the postman's knock without a quickening of the heart. For who can bear to feel himself forgotten?…

Mardling and a Troshin' to the End

My Old Cat – By Hal Summers

My old cat is dead, who would butt me with his head, he had the sleekest fur, he had the blackest purr, always gentle with us was the black puss, but when I found him today stiff and cold where he lay his look was a lion's, full of rage, defiance, oh, he would not pretend that what came was a friend but met it in pure hate. Well died, my old cat.

Norfolk – By Michael O'Neill

Sand-martins whirling out of cliffs. Hay trussed in roly-poly bales. Stalled windmills. Big skies. A place for weather-watching rites, for money to invest in, rewarding itself with the obligatory boat and a lawn that tapers off in search of water, life's elixir, leisure's mirror. Walsingham and Cromer: the manufactured shrine with something - nothingness? - candled at its heart, the deft resort with one eye on your wallet and one on the enigma of the sky that bends above the threatened beach where if, as they heap and spill, drag and heap, the waves are trying to communicate - some maxim, perhaps concerning survival, the need to endure, to hope just enough - you find you're baffled, you can't hear a word.

The Coast: Norfolk – By Frances Cornford

As on the highway's quiet edge he mows the grass beside the hedge, the old man has for company the distant, grey, salt-smelling sea, a poppied field, a cow and calf, the finches on the telegraph. Across his faded back a hone, he slowly, slowly scythes alone in silence of the wind-soft air, with ladies' bedstraw everywhere, with whitened corn, and tarry poles, and far-off gulls like risen souls…

Mardling and a Troshin' to the End

Watercolour Painting Of Queen Boudica by the Author…

A Norfolk Hero: Boudica, an Ode: By William Cowper

When the British warrior queen, bleeding from the Roman rods, sought with and indignant mien, counsel of her country's gods, sage beneath a spreading oak sat the Druid, hoary chief, ev'ry burning word he spoke, full of rage and full of grief.
Princess! if our aged eyes weep upon thy matchless wrongs, 'tis because resentment ties all the terrors of our tongues. Rome shall perish - write that word In the blood that she has spilt; perish hopeless and abhorr'd, deep in ruin as in guilt.

Rome for empire far renown'd, tramples on a thousand states, soon her pride shall kiss the ground - Hark! the Gaul is at her gates. Other Romans shall arise, heedless of a soldier's name, sounds, not arms, shall win the prize, harmony the path to fame. Then the progeny that springs form the forests of our land, arm'd with thunder, clad with wings, shall a wider world command. Regions Caesar never knew, thy posterity shall sway, where his eagles never flew, none invincible as they.

Such the bard's prophetic words, pregnant with celestial fire, bending as he swept the chords of his sweet but awful lyre. She with all a monarch's pride, felt them in her bosom glow, rush'd to battle, fought and died, dying, hurl'd them at the foe. Ruffians, pittiless as proud, heav'n awards the vengeance due, empire is on us bestow'd shame and ruin wait for you…

Mardling and a Troshin' to the End

Alan an
Old Norfolk Boy…

I know that I am Getting Old - By Alan R. Massen

I know that I am getting old, when things that I have enjoyed are no more involved, when things are a fading memory of joy and passion, as foreign Greek shores beckon me no more.

I know that I am getting old, when my knee joints are no longer my own, made from alien steel not bone, I totter on staggering steps with a heavy heart, I await my fate, as the surgeon, when weight permits, once more will replace my knees with alien metal joints.

I know that I am getting old, when losing weight is what I am told, the surgeon says I am too heavy for going under his knife, and states that my cigarettes smoking days are to be no more, it is starting to feel to me as if all may be lost after all.

I know that I am getting old, as I wave farewell to my old friend, my car, which has served me so very well but it has to go, it has been with me so very long but now it must sadly go.

I know that I am getting old, as my memories are now full of all that I have known, but whilst my brain keeps working well and I can go, in my mind, wherever I want to go, I am almost pain free, without any add on wheels, being bionic in steel.

I know that I am getting old, with less than nibble joints I am told and maybe I am not as fit as could be, but with no shortness of breath so I can be happy and content to be an old Norfolk boy who will go a **Mardling and a Troshin' in Norfolk to my End** in the place I love best.

Just before we leave we will in the last chapter of this book we will be enjoying a selection of **My 2020 Artworks**…

My 2020 Artworks

Susie and fishing boats in Skiathos Town - by Alan R Massen 2020

Alan at the Troulos Bay Hotel at lunchtime - by Alan R Massen 2020

More of my 2020 Artworks to follow…

My 2020 Artworks

Our Charlie in our Norfolk garden - by Alan R Massen 2020

Our Poppy in the snow - by Alan R Massen 2020

More of my 2020 Artworks to follow…

My 2020 Artworks

Across the rooftops of Skiathos Town - by Alan R Massen 2020

Alan all at sea off Skiathos - by Alan R Massen 2020

More of my 2020 Artworks to follow…

My 2020 Artworks

All in a line on the island of Crete - by Alan R Massen 2020

All in a line on Corfu - by Alan R Massen 2020

More of my 2020 Artworks to follow…

My 2020 Artworks

All rolled up in Norfolk - by Alan R Massen 2020

Along the beach at Cromer in Norfolk - by Alan R Massen 2020

More of my 2020 Artworks to follow…

My 2020 Artworks

Baby fawn in a Norfolk wood with it's Mum - by Alan R Massen 2020

An alley cat in Skiathos Town - by Alan R Massen 2020

More of my 2020 Artworks to follow…

My 2020 Artworks

Beach huts at Wells Next the Sea - by Alan R Massen 2020

Beach huts at Wells Next the Sea in Norfolk - by Alan R Massen 2020

More of my 2020 Artworks to follow…

My 2020 Artworks

Boat leaving the island of Skyros - by Alan R Massen 2020

Boat and shades on Troulos Bay beach - by Alan R Massen 2020

More of my 2020 Artworks to follow…

My 2020 Artworks

Boats at Assos on Kefalonia - by Alan R Massen 2020

Boats at Blakeney in Norfolk - by Alan R Massen 2020

More of my 2020 Artworks to follow…

My 2020 Artworks

Boats in Mousehole harbour - by Alan R Massen 2020

Boats at shipwreck beach on Zakynthos - by Alan R Massen 2020

More of my 2020 Artworks to follow…

My 2020 Artworks

Boats in port on the island of Ithaca - by Alan R Massen 2020

Boats in Troulos Bay on Skiathos - by Alan R Massen 2020

More of my 2020 Artworks to follow…

My 2020 Artworks

Boats, sea and mountains on Thassos - by Alan R Massen 2020

Bringing the catch home - by Alan R Massen 2020

More of my 2020 Artworks to follow…

My 2020 Artworks

Susie on Portinatx beach on Ibiza - by Alan R Massen 2020

Cat napping - by Alan R Massen 2020

More of my 2020 Artworks to follow…

My 2020 Artworks

Coming into land on Skiathos - by Alan R Massen 2020

Church on the hill in Skiathos Town - by Alan R Massen 2020

More of my 2020 Artworks to follow…

My 2020 Artworks

Cornish fishing boat off Cornwall - by Alan R Massen 2020

Coming into Zakynthos Town harbour - by Alan R Massen 2020

More of my 2020 Artworks to follow…

My 2020 Artworks

Susie and Poppy in our garden - by Alan R Massen 2020

Alan in the Mythos Cafe on Skiathos - by Alan R Massen 2020

More of my 2020 Artworks to follow…

My 2020 Artworks

Down the steps to a church on Santorini - by Alan R Massen 2020

Donkeys on the island of Hydra - by Alan R Massen 2020

More of my 2020 Artworks to follow…

My 2020 Artworks

Susie on Troulos Bay beach on Skiathos - by Alan R Massen 2020

Fawn hiding in the long grass - by Alan R Massen 2020

More of my 2020 Artworks to follow…

My 2020 Artworks

Fishing boat in Zakynthos Town port - by Alan R Massen 2020

Fishing boat at Porto Roxa on Zakynthos - by Alan R Massen 2020

More of my 2020 Artworks to follow…

My 2020 Artworks

Fishing boats at Fiskardo on Kefalonia - by Alan R Massen 2020

Floating in Zakynthos Town - by Alan R Massen 2020

More of my 2020 Artworks to follow…

My 2020 Artworks

Fishing boats in Skiathos Town bay - by Alan R Massen 2020

Fishing boats in Skiathos Town old port - by Alan R Massen 2020

More of my 2020 Artworks to follow…

My 2020 Artworks

Flowers all in a line in our garden - by Alan R Massen 2020

Flowers blooming in our Norfolk garden - by Alan R Massen 2020

More of my 2020 Artworks to follow…

My 2020 Artworks

Flying over Norfolk bluebells - by Alan R Massen 2020

Fox alert and ready for action - by Alan R Massen 2020

More of my 2020 Artworks to follow…

My 2020 Artworks

Fox cub with his mum - by Alan R Massen 2020

Fox enjoying a rest - by Alan R Massen 2020

More of my 2020 Artworks to follow…

My 2020 Artworks

Frappe time on the island of Skiathos - by Alan R Massen 2020

Fox on a rainy day in Norfolk - by Alan R Massen 2020

More of my 2020 Artworks to follow…

My 2020 Artworks

Alan in the old port in Skiathos Town - by Alan R Massen 2020

Susie in shades on the island of Kefalonia - by Alan R Massen 2020

More of my 2020 Artworks to follow…

My 2020 Artworks

Goat on a hill on the island of Kefalonia - by Alan R Massen 2020

Give me the honey mummy - by Alan R Massen 2020

More of my 2020 Artworks to follow…

My 2020 Artworks

Greek tragedy masks - by Alan R Massen 2020

Greek tragedy mask being used in Athens - by Alan R Massen 2020

More of my 2020 Artworks to follow…

My 2020 Artworks

Greyhound racing - by Alan R Massen 2020

Green is the colour - by Alan R Massen 2020

More of my 2020 Artworks to follow…

My 2020 Artworks

Harbour on the island of Crete - by Alan R Massen 2020

Harbour, town and castle on Ibiza - by Alan R Massen 2020

More of my 2020 Artworks to follow…

My 2020 Artworks

Harry working on Skiathos - by Alan R Massen 2020

Hotel lounge on the island of Zakynthos - by Alan R Massen 2020

More of my 2020 Artworks to follow…

My 2020 Artworks

Harvest bales in a Norfolk field - by Alan R Massen 2020

Hare in the long grass - by Alan R Massen 2020

More of my 2020 Artworks to follow…

My 2020 Artworks

Horse hiding in a Norfolk reed bed - by Alan R Massen 2020

Herd of deer in winter - by Alan R Massen 2020

More of my 2020 Artworks to follow…

My 2020 Artworks

In loving memory of Franky - by Alan R Massen 2020

In the bleak mid-winter - by Alan R Massen 2020

More of my 2020 Artworks to follow…

My 2020 Artworks

Kingfisher flying home with tea - by Alan R Massen 2020

In the nets in the old port in Skiathos Town - by Alan R Massen 2020

More of my 2020 Artworks to follow…

My 2020 Artworks

Alan on the Greek island of Ithaca - by Alan R Massen 2020

Susie in hat and shades on Troulos Bay beach - by Alan R Massen 2020

More of my 2020 Artworks to follow…

My 2020 Artworks

Kingfisher on the lookout - by Alan R Massen 2020

Kingfisher resting in the Norfolk landscape - by Alan R Massen 2020

More of my 2020 Artworks to follow…

My 2020 Artworks

Lowering the baulks into Mousehole harbour - by Alan R Massen 2020

Lavender in our Norfolk garden - by Alan R Massen 2020

More of my 2020 Artworks to follow…

My 2020 Artworks

Susie onboard off Skiathos - by Alan R Massen 2020

Mum in shades and a hat - by Alan R Massen 2020

More of my 2020 Artworks to follow…

My 2020 Artworks

Misty morning on the Norfolk Broads - by Alan R Massen 2020

Marble in our Norfolk garden - by Alan R Massen 2020

More of my 2020 Artworks to follow…

My 2020 Artworks

Minoans sailing away from Thera - by Alan R Massen 2020

Mending the nets in Thassos Town - by Alan R Massen 2020

More of my 2020 Artworks to follow…

My 2020 Artworks

Mousehole harbour in Cornwall - by Alan R Massen 2020

My bleeding heart in our Norfolk garden - by Alan R Massen 2020

More of my 2020 Artworks to follow…

My 2020 Artworks

Susie in Portinatx on Ibiza - by Alan R Massen 2020

Alan saying Yammas from Skiathos Town - by Alan R Massen 2020

More of my 2020 Artworks to follow…

My 2020 Artworks

Olympic runners in Skiathos Town - by Alan R Massen 2020

Our Norfolk garden - by Alan R Massen 2020

More of my 2020 Artworks to follow…

My 2020 Artworks

More of my 2020 Artworks to follow…

My 2020 Artworks

Our Poppy on the lookout at Shouldham Warren - by Alan R Massen

Peacock flashing it's tail feathers - by Alan R Massen 2020

More of my 2020 Artworks to follow…

My 2020 Artworks

Camel parking in the City of Cairo - by Alan R Massen 2020

Out and about in Skiathos Town - by Alan R Massen 2020

More of my 2020 Artworks to follow…

My 2020 Artworks

Port on the Greek island of Crete - by Alan R Massen 2020

Priest walking in Skiathos Town - by Alan R Massen 2020

More of my 2020 Artworks to follow…

My 2020 Artworks

Racing after the hare - by Alan R Massen 2020

Susie on a rock at Portinatx on Ibiza - by Alan R Massen 2020

More of my 2020 Artworks to follow…

My 2020 Artworks

Rainbow over the Parthenon in Athens - by Alan R Massen 2020

Roadside shrine on Crete - by Alan R Massen 2020

More of my 2020 Artworks to follow…

My 2020 Artworks

Riding towards the Great Pyramid of Giza - by Alan R Massen 2020

Rocks on the island of Cyprus - by Alan R Massen 2020

More of my 2020 Artworks to follow…

My 2020 Artworks

Sa Coma beach on Majorca - by Alan R Massen 2020

Rocks, dolphin and seascape on Cyprus - by Alan R Massen 2020

More of my 2020 Artworks to follow…

My 2020 Artworks

Sailing away from the Norfolk coast - by Alan R Massen 2020

Seal in the North Sea off Norfolk - by Alan R Massen 2020

More of my 2020 Artworks to follow…

My 2020 Artworks

Shades in the sea on Crete - by Alan R Massen 2020

Shades by the sea on Skiathos - by Alan R Massen 2020

More of my 2020 Artworks to follow…

My 2020 Artworks

Spartan helmet of ancient Greece - by Alan R Massen 2020

Spread your wings and fly away - by Alan R Massen 2020

More of my 2020 Artworks to follow…

My 2020 Artworks

Standing proud in Norfolk - by Alan R Massen 2020

Sheep on the road near Edale - by Alan R Massen 2020

More of my 2020 Artworks to follow…

My 2020 Artworks

Standing in the old port in Skiathos Town - by Alan R Massen 2020

Sunbeds and shades on Troulos Bay beach - by Alan R Massen 2020

More of my 2020 Artworks to follow…

My 2020 Artworks

Sunset on Mousehole harbour - by Alan R Massen 2020

Sunset on (Mumma Mia) church on Skopelos - by Alan R Massen 2020

More of my 2020 Artworks to follow…

My 2020 Artworks

Sunset on Santorini - by Alan R Massen 2020

Sunset over Cairo in Egypt - by Alan R Massen 2020

More of my 2020 Artworks to follow…

My 2020 Artworks

Sunset on the Norfolk Broads - by Alan R Massen 2020

Susie in Vathy on Ithaca - by Alan R Massen 2020

More of my 2020 Artworks to follow…

My 2020 Artworks

Tables and chairs on the island of Mykonos - by Alan R Massen 2020

Taverna by the sea on Thassos - by Alan R Massen 2020

More of my 2020 Artworks to follow…

My 2020 Artworks

Taverna on the island of Zakynthos - by Alan R Massen 2020

Taverna on the Greek island of Serifos - by Alan R Massen 2020

More of my 2020 Artworks to follow…

My 2020 Artworks

The harbour at Mousehole in Cornwall - by Alan R Massen 2020

The front garden of our Norfolk home - by Alan R Massen 2020

More of my 2020 Artworks to follow…

My 2020 Artworks

The Hydra from Greek mythology - by Alan R Massen 2020

The Kiss - by Alan R Massen 2020

More of my 2020 Artworks to follow…

My 2020 Artworks

The little people in our garden - by Alan R Massen 2020

The night owl - by Alan R Massen 2020

More of my 2020 Artworks to follow…

My 2020 Artworks

The paradise island of Mykonos - by Alan R Massen 2020

The Sphinx and the Great Pyramid at Giza - by Alan R Massen 2020

More of my 2020 Artworks to follow…

My 2020 Artworks

More of my 2020 Artworks to follow…

My 2020 Artworks

The village of Assos on Kefalonia - by Alan R Massen 2020

The statue in the old port in Skiathos Town - by Alan R Massen 2020

More of my 2020 Artworks to follow…

My 2020 Artworks

Town on the Greek island of Zakynthos - by Alan R Massen 2020

Upside down cat - by Alan R Massen 2020

More of my 2020 Artworks to follow…

My 2020 Artworks

Waves onto a quayside on Crete - by Alan R Massen 2020

Walkway out into the sea on Zakynthos - by Alan R Massen 2020

More of my 2020 Artworks to follow…

My 2020 Artworks

Wells Next the Sea harbour quay in Norfolk - by Alan R Massen 2020

Windmill in the Norfolk reeds - by Alan R Massen 2020

More of my 2020 Artworks to follow…

My 2020 Artworks

Windmills on the Greek island of Mykonos - by Alan R Massen 2020

Windmill on the Spanish island of Mallorca - by Alan R Massen 2020

More of my 2020 Artworks to follow…

My 2020 Artworks

Yacht and islet off Zakynthos - by Alan R Massen 2020

Winter hide and seek - by Alan R Massen 2020

More of my 2020 Artworks to follow…

My 2020 Artworks

Zeus the Lion - by Alan R Massen 2020

Zebra having a dust bath - by Alan R Massen 2020

More of my 2020 Artworks to follow…

My 2020 Artworks

Susie sailing off the island of Kefalonia - by Alan R Massen 2020

Alan waving from the Troulos Bay Hotel - by Alan R Massen 2020

THE END

Acknowledgement

I would like to acknowledge and thank ALL the people of Norfolk and specifically the following: Lord Horatio Nelson, Allan Smethurst, John Kett, James Wentworth Day, Bernard E. Dorman, John Betjeman, Alan Savory, Hal Summers, Michael O'Neill, Walter de la Mare, John McCrae, Roger McGough, W.H.Auden, Frances Cornford,William Cowper, Cameron Self, Johnny Cash, Arthur H. Patterson, William Riviere, Anon, Marshall and W.A. Duff for all their great written works that have inspired me so much over the last seventy years. Thank you also to my friends, family and my orthopaedic surgeon Mr. James Jeffery FRCS who have all helped make me what I am today. Finally a big thank you must go to my publisher Rainbow Publications UK for supporting me in the publishing of my books.

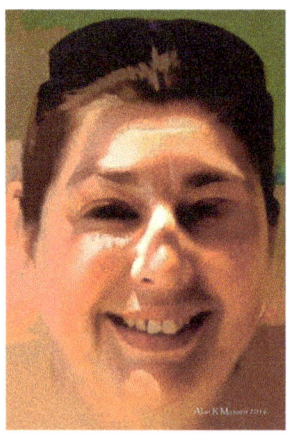  

I believe that the most important thing to ensure that you live and enjoy your life to the full is to have someone to share your experiences and memories with. I am lucky I have my wife and best friend Susie as my companion and her smile and enthusiasm has made every day of our time together very special, enjoyable and full of love. Long may it continue. So until the next time we meet happy Mardling and a Troshin wherever you are!

Copyright © 2020 Alan R. Massen

www.ingramcontent.com/pod-product-compliance
Lightning Source LLC
Chambersburg PA
CBHW042227010526
44113CB00045B/2836